PRAISE FOR GUIDE TO AN EXTRAORDINARY LIFE

"With pastoral insight, engaging storytelling, and inspirational clarity, Deacon Greg Kandra unpacks the extraordinary wisdom of the two greatest commandments. *The Busy Person's Guide to an Extraordinary Life* is full of the everyday wisdom we need to truly live our calling as saints in the making. Deacon Greg has long been one of my go-to mentors for living a faith-filled life, and this book reminds me why!"
—LISA M. HENDEY, author of *I Am God's Storyteller*

"Like a spiritual memoir, Deacon Greg Kandra's new book is quintessential storytelling by a master, framed by Scripture, prayer, and reflection leading to faith in action. It is profoundly moving and delightfully uplifting."
—SR. ROSE PACATTE, FSP, film critic for the *National Catholic Reporter* and *St. Anthony Messenger*

"I've never heard Deacon Greg Kandra preach, but this book has convinced me he'd be a joy to listen to. He tells a good story. He keeps it simple. And at the same time he leaves the reader feeling that an extraordinary life is within grasp if we just pay a bit closer attention to God and our neighbor."
—GREG ERLANDSON, director and editor-in-chief, Catholic News Service

"How can I live the life that Jesus calls me to live? According to him, it's a matter of loving God and loving my neighbor. While it sounds simple in theory, I'm constantly distracted by the busyness and complexity of life and often fail to put it into practice. In *The Busy Person's Guide to an Extraordinary Life*, Deacon Greg Kandra gives me practical steps to follow and reminds me that even I can lead an extraordinary life. I've been waiting for this book!"
—**GARY ZIMAK,** bestselling author, speaker, and radio host

THE BUSY

PERSON'S GUIDE TO

AN EXTRA ORDINARY LIFE

**DEACON
GREG KANDRA**

Published by The Word Among Us Press
7115 Guilford Drive, Suite 100
Frederick, Maryland 21704
wau.org

24 23 22 21 20   1 2 3 4 5

ISBN: 978-1-59325-513-8
eISBN: 978-1-59325-514-5

Nihil obstat: The Reverend Michael Morgan, J.D., J.C.
Censor Librorum
August 24, 2020

Imprimatur: +Most Reverend Felipe J. Estévez, S.T.D.
Bishop of St. Augustine
August 24, 2020

"Afterword: The World Turned Upside Down" is adapted from an essay that appeared on the website for *The Deacon* magazine in April 2020.

Design by Suzanne Earl

Made and printed in the United States of America

Library of Congress Control Number: 2020916144

For Karen, my extraordinary sister, with gratitude and love.

CONTENTS

INTRODUCTION

In 1980, one of the biggest and most powerful organizations in the world thought it could use a little publicity. It decided to launch an advertising campaign.

So it hired a copywriter by the name of Earl Carter, who came up with an idea that was so simple—yet so powerful and captivating—that the slogan instantly caught on.

It's now the stuff of legends. In 1999, the publication *Advertising Age* named it one of the best advertising campaigns of the twentieth century. In fact, it is considered such an important part of American history that Carter's concept sheet—the notepad containing that phrase—is preserved in the permanent collection of a museum. And it has endured. The big client ended up using the campaign and its slogan for over two decades.

Earl Carter's client was the US Army. And his slogan? "Be All You Can Be."

Aside from being an intriguing part of advertising lore—and a fascinating, largely overlooked chapter in American military history—that simple phrase resonates in ways all of us recognize. It could almost stand as the eleventh commandment for people of faith. There, in five short words, you have everything that God calls us to do, every aspiration he asks us to achieve, every expectation or desire or dream he might have for every one of us.

"There," he says, as he breathes us into existence. "Now be all you can be."

Well, sure. That's easy for *him* to say.

What about the rest of us?

How do we go about actually fulfilling that?

Looked at another way: how can we not only live up to our expectations (or God's) but also make of our lives something out of the ordinary?

How do you live an extraordinary life?

It may not be as hard as you think. And in reality, it's not really a secret.

Look no further than St. Matthew's Gospel:

When the Pharisees heard that he had silenced the Sadducees, they gathered together, and one of them [a scholar of the law] tested him by asking, "Teacher, which commandment in the law is the greatest?" He said to him, "You shall love the Lord, your God, with all your heart, with all your soul, and with all your mind. This is the greatest and the first commandment. The second is like it: You shall love your neighbor as yourself. The whole law and the prophets depend on these two commandments."
—22:34-40

There it is, hiding in plain sight: love the Lord, and love your neighbor.

Of course, if it were that simple, the rest of the pages in this book would be blank.

The fact is, actually fulfilling those mandates—"the two great commandments"—is a challenge. It is so easy to become lax, complacent, indifferent. We take God for granted. We take *one another* for granted. We fumble. We fall.

Face it: we sin.

It becomes even harder in the manic, frenetic age in which we live—when the distractions of email, texting, television, and multiple deadlines on all fronts make muddling through every day a chore. And let's not even talk about praying; who has time for *that*? (Oddly enough, I wrote a book about that: *The Busy Person's Guide to Prayer*.) Can't we just be good people, be kind to one another, and let it go at that?

Well, sure. If you want your life to be, you know, *ordinary*.

But there is so much more that we can do and that we can *be*.

"The ways of the Lord are not easy," Pope Benedict told German pilgrims to the Vatican in 2005, "but we were not created for an easy life, but for great things, for goodness."[1]

We were created for something extraordinary.

And that brings us to the book you're holding in your hands. In the chapters to come, I will offer some ideas on how we can help realize that—and transcend the ordinary—using as our guide those two great commandments. We'll look at how God expresses his love for us (whether we are aware of it or not) and consider some ways we can respond to that love, and we'll talk about our love for our neighbor and how to live out that love. I'll suggest things we can do every day that require little more than our own human desire, a yearning from the heart. You may be surprised to find you are doing some of them already, in one way or another—and isn't that wonderful to discover?

This book is divided into two sections for the two commandments we're going to be exploring. That, I hope, will help give some focus and organization to the often unfocused and disorganized process of thinking about God (and writing about him!).

Since I'm hardly the definitive authority on the subject, at the end of every chapter, I'll include a quote from a well-known person and a brief reflection from people who are mostly unknown—friends and colleagues of mine who have a way of making these notions tangible and explicit and real. Each chapter concludes with a prayer.

I've done my best to keep the accompanying chapters brief and easily digestible. You could read a chapter a day, if you like, without breaking a sweat, or you could delve right in and read the whole thing in one sitting. It's a little book because it's a book for busy people, and I know you have other things to do.

But nothing could matter more than becoming our best— for ourselves, for our neighbors and, above all, for God. The idea behind this book is that no matter what we have to *do*, we have so much that we are called to *be*.

God's challenge to us all couldn't be simpler—or more daunting.

Go ahead, he says. *I've given you life. Now be all you can be.*

PART 1

HOW GOD LOVES US—AND WE LOVE HIM

CHAPTER 1

TELL ME A STORY

As the Father loves me, so I also love you.
Remain in my love.
—John 15:9

Years ago, the PBS series *American Masters* profiled a former colleague of mine from CBS News: the late great Don Hewitt.

Among his many accomplishments in a legendary life, Don was the creator and executive producer of *60 Minutes*—one of the longest running, most acclaimed programs in television history.

At one point in this documentary, the producer asked Hewitt, "What is the secret of the show's success? How has it endured for over thirty years?"

"It comes down to four little words," Don told her, "words that every child knows: "Tell me a story.""

It's just that simple, he said. Every week, people tune in and want that. And, he admitted, *60 Minutes* has mastered the art of storytelling.

The fact is: we are a storytelling people. It's woven into our DNA. What started in caves around a fire now happens in living rooms around a TV screen or—increasingly—in

Starbucks around a laptop or on buses and trains with a cell phone in our hands. We have this insatiable need to pass on what we have seen, what we have heard, what we have experienced, what we know. We want to tell stories.

Don Hewitt's answer in that documentary got me wondering: when it comes to sharing the Christian message with the world, what story are we telling?

Whether we realize it or not, the story we are commissioned to tell the world is a *love* story. The great Christian story—what has been called, famously, the greatest story ever told—is the story of God's love for us, our love for him, and our shared love for one another in a world where, to be honest, love is often lacking.

We often forget that love is where it all begins. And we are poorer because we forget.

Years ago, a deacon classmate of mine shared a story with me about his Mass of Thanksgiving, celebrated the day after he was ordained. He'd prepared his homily, practiced it, fine-tuned it. He'd worked out the kinks, smoothed over the transitions, made his punchy and pious points in all the right ways.

Just before Mass, the pastor asked him, in the sacristy, if he was ready.

"Oh yeah," my friend replied. "Ready to go."

"And your homily?"

"It's all set."

"Good," the pastor replied. "Good. Good luck." And he took a breath and offered some final words of wisdom. "Just remember this," he said gently. "Whatever you tell 'em, just make sure you tell 'em God loves 'em."

It seems like an obvious statement, and it sounded so obvious to me. Well, yeah. Okay. God loves you. Don't people know that?

Spoiler alert: not really. Too many don't realize that everything we are, everything we profess to believe, begins with love.

If my years in ministry have taught me anything, it's this sobering truth: a surprising number of people don't believe they are loved or—more significantly—that they are lovable. In turn, they have a hard time loving. We live in a wounded world, with wounded people who have been shunned, ignored, kicked around, or just dismissed. So many of us have the bruises to show for it. That, sadly, is life.

I hear it from people after Mass, and from couples seeking an annulment. More and more, faithful Catholics come from broken homes and carry broken hearts. (Statistics tell us Catholics divorce at about the same rate as everyone else.) As a result, they look at the world with suspicion or cynicism or mistrust. They are gossiped about or passed over for promotions or betrayed by petty (or sometimes not so petty) infidelities at work, at home—in relationships of all kinds.

And they then find themselves in a pew on Sunday morning, praying words of humility, penance and remorse—"I confess to almighty God and to you, my brothers and sisters, that I have greatly sinned"—and they can't help but feel, for whatever reason, unfit.

So it's no small wonder that the Gospel message that resonates the most with so many, the one that bandages the bruises and makes them feel whole again, is one that reminds them that they are loved. To be reminded of that can be more than encouraging; it can be overwhelming. It might even be lifesaving.

To hear anew that Jesus gave his life for them, for *us*, or to hear again about Christ's healing miracles or simply to sit and reflect on that familiar passage from the Gospel of John— "For God so loved the world that he gave his only Son, so that everyone who believes in him might not perish but might have eternal life" (3:16)—is like a dose of B$_{12}$ to a weary disciple.

I've lost count of the number of times parishioners have stopped me after Mass to say a word about a homily I'd preached about God's love and then add, quietly, "I really needed that." For a long time, I was surprised because I didn't think I was telling them anything new or sharing something they didn't already experience.

But in time, I came to realize I was wrong. That wise pastor knew what he was talking about. It remains the single best piece of advice I've heard about preaching.

"Whatever you tell 'em, just make sure you tell 'em God loves 'em."

We do need that. Really. Especially now, when so much of the world is telling us we aren't rich enough, powerful enough, attractive enough, successful enough, fit enough. God cuts through the clutter to tell us that bold, counter-cultural truth: the world is wrong.

And we are loved. *You* are loved.

Still unconvinced? Check the Bible. It's there in black and white.

"From afar the LORD appears: / With age-old love I have loved you" (Jeremiah 31:3).

"See what love the Father has bestowed on us that we may be called the children of God. Yet so we are" (1 John 3:1).

"In this is love: not that we have loved God, but that he loved us and sent his Son as expiation for our sins. Beloved, if God so loved us, we also must love one another" (1 John 4:10-11).

I could go on. But you get the drift. (A little later I'll look at some of the more concrete, extravagantly wondrous ways God expresses his love for us—whether we are aware of it or not. He is full of surprises.)

So if we are indeed loved by God—and yes, we are!—we can do nothing less than love him in return and express that love not only to him but to his single greatest creative achievement, our brothers and sisters in the world. The two great commandments—love of God, love of neighbor—are closely entwined. Both express our deep gratitude to the Creator and his ultimate creation; one could even argue that you can't fully love one without loving the other.

And from that comes something breathtakingly close to joy: an extraordinary life.

CONSIDER THIS

You are good and all-powerful, caring for each one of us as though each is the only one in your care.

—St. Augustine[2]

The philosopher Kierkegaard once said, "It is quite true . . . that life must be understood backward. But . . . it must be *lived forward*."[3] That's exactly how I see my knowledge and understanding of God's love: it has been most clearly revealed as I reflect over the years gone by.

Looking back, I marvel at how God has revealed his love for me over the course of my lifetime. In fact, my understanding of his love has been an evolution. I saw his loving presence in the faces of my newborn children and grandchildren, in the pastoral needs of my students and their families, in the laughter I shared with my friends, in the joy of marriage, and now in the retired life that my husband and I share in South Florida.

Both in the good times and in the bad, God has sustained me through his grace and mercy. When I faced the challenges of raising three young children and trying to make ends meet while teaching full time, God never left me to fend for myself alone. He always sent someone to cheer me or provide clarity and hope and kindness. That meant so much to me.

I too try to offer a smile and some encouraging words to others. In our current times, people are often overwhelmed and need to hear that they are doing a good job in spite of the many challenges they are facing.

I am reminded of the poem "Footprints in the Sand." God explains why there was only one set of footprints during the most troublesome times of the poet's life: "My precious, precious child. I love you, and I would never, never leave you during your times of trial and suffering. When you saw only one set of footprints, it was then that I carried you."

In response to God's loving presence in my life, I choose each day to respond intentionally:

- To pray often, attend Mass frequently, and meditate on the wonder of this life.
- To speak less; to listen and reflect more.
- To practice gratitude by realizing and counting my blessings.
- To be present in the moment. Listen to the birds singing. Watch the trees swaying in the breeze. Smell the flowers in my garden. Look for the rainbow while it rains.
- To share a warm smile or a kind word with those I encounter each day.
- To always remember that God is good . . . all the time!
  —Patti Murphy Dohn, North Palm Beach, Florida

TRY THIS

A popular method of prayer at the end of the day is a simple examination of conscience—searching our hearts to examine the events of the day, the choices we've made, the things we have done, the things we have left undone. But I suggest that another fruitful way to look at our lives—and come to a deeper appreciation of God's work in our lives—is an examination of gifts.

What has God given me this day to help me carry out his will?

What am I thankful for?

How have I seen God today? How have I felt his love for me and those around me? What have I seen or heard that touched me, reassured me, inspired me, changed me?

Directing our hearts this way, with prayer and a humble but grateful spirit, can help us become attuned to God's work in the world.

It might also help us to cultivate an attitude of gratitude, to never take anything or anyone for granted, and to see our lives as God's ultimate expression of love for each of us.

PRAY THIS

Oh good and gracious God,
help me to see anew what you have given me.
When my heart has been darkened by doubt,
give me the light of another sunrise;
when my soul has grown weary with worry,
send a friend with hands to lift, to hold, to help bear the weight;
when I forget what you have done for me,
help me to remember.
Help me to remember it all.
Draw me closer to you when I drift away,
and keep me always near.
Forgive me for the times I've been forgetful of you.

Have patience with me, your fumbling and struggling child,
so that I can continue to learn and to grow—always growing deeper in my love for you
and all you have given me.
Your love is everywhere, if only I take the time to see it.
Amen.

CHAPTER 2

WHERE DO WE FIND GOD?

Hear, O Israel! The LORD is our God, the LORD alone!
Therefore, you shall love the LORD, your God,
with your whole heart, and with your whole being,
and with your whole strength.
—Deuteronomy 6:4-5

If we want to talk about God's abiding love for us, a great place to begin is with the very center of our faith: the Eucharist. There you will find the gift that keeps on giving.

Think about it: at every Mass, Christ becomes present to us under the meager appearance of bread and wine so that we can receive him and take him with us and within us out into the world. And it happens again and again, in chapels and cathedrals and basements and churches and hospitals and pitched tents, all over the globe. It has been this way for two millennia, and it will go on until there is no more time to count.

Mass is probably the most familiar way we Catholics gather to worship, adore, and express our love for God and receive him in Holy Communion. But I'd like us to think too about another way that is too often neglected or over-looked. Even its very name sums up what we are there to do: it is the simple but profound act of Adoration of the Blessed Sacrament.

We have weekly Adoration at my parish in Queens, and it's rare to find more than a handful of people gathered there at any given time. Do people know what they are missing? To pray before the Blessed Sacrament, even for just a few minutes, is to engage in an intimate conversation with the One who made us.

The *Catechism* describes it this way:

> *Adoration* is the first attitude of man acknowledging that he is a creature before his Creator. It exalts the greatness of the Lord who made us and the almighty power of the Savior who sets us free from evil. Adoration is homage of the spirit to the "King of Glory," respectful silence in the presence of the "ever greater" God. Adoration of the thrice-holy and sovereign God of love blends with humility and gives assurance to our supplications. (2628)

Beyond the profound theological implications of all this, there is this confounding fact: it all begins with bread. Could anything be more basic or humble?

When I was young and first living on my own, way back before I was married, I decided to try to teach myself to cook. The "man-sized" TV dinners weren't cutting it. So I got a couple of cookbooks, including one called *Cooking for Men*, which included recipes for things like meat loaf, chili, and pot roast.

But the most adventurous thing I attempted was baking bread. I don't know why I thought this was something I needed to know how to do, but I decided to give it a shot. If you've ever tried this, you know it's an all-day affair. You mix the ingredients and knead the dough and then you knead it again and then you have to wait for it to rise and then you have to actually bake it.

It took hours. I told a friend about it later. He listened very politely and then replied, earnestly: "You know, Greg, you don't have to do that. They sell that already made at Safeway. It's in little plastic bags. It's called Wonder Bread. You should try it."

That was more or less the beginning and end of my career as a baker.

Nevertheless, just-baked bread is a wonder. The smell, the texture, and even the flavor is unlike anything in the world. And if you add butter or jelly or even use fresh bread to make a sandwich, well, it's transformative. It is truly astounding to consider what bread can become.

That is something to remember when we consider "the source and summit" of our Catholic faith: the Eucharist—it is astounding to consider what bread can become (*Catechism*, 1324; *Lumen Gentium*, 11).

The work it takes to bake a loaf of bread can't begin to compare with what has gone into creating the Eucharist. It is the labor of a lifetime—Jesus' lifetime. All that he taught and lived and suffered and died has been poured into that sanctifying moment when bread becomes his Body. By the hands of the priest and the grace of God, the mundane becomes a miracle.

It is more than just transubstantiation—that massive word the nuns taught us in grade school that describes what happens on the altar. It is nothing less than a resounding echo of the Incarnation.

It has been said that God became man so that man might become God. In the miracle of the Eucharist, we experience it and relive it.

Yes, it is astounding to consider what bread can become. It is a miracle and a mystery, yet it continues to happen.

What began on Holy Thursday with a few people around a table now feeds multitudes around the world. Jesus continues to give—and give us himself—under the appearance of bread.

Which is why devoted people around the world find a reason to visit church, sit in a pew, and gaze up at a monstrance containing the Body of Christ. "O come, let us adore him," the celebrated Christmas carol tells us, "O come, let us adore him, Christ the Lord." Christ is there, Body and Blood, Soul and Divinity.

Visiting God this way, spending time in Adoration, is about as close as we can come to visiting the newborn Jesus in Bethlehem—the little town whose very name, of course, means House of Bread.

But what if you can't get to Adoration or can't find a church offering Adoration? What if you are miles away from the nearest monstrance containing a Host? Or—more pointedly—what if you are too busy? What if your schedule is too crowded to take the time to shut out the world and spend some quality time with God?

When I was studying to become a deacon, one of my best friends was my classmate Jim Hynes. Jim was a big, burly guy, a retired cop. By nature and disposition, he was a gentle giant. We bonded when we realized we both shared a great enthusiasm for all things Disney. He loved Disney World, and for a big man, his favorite Disney character was one of the smallest: Jiminy Cricket from *Pinocchio*.

About ten months after we were ordained, Jim was rushed to the hospital. They found cancer and tried to treat it. But he also had heart trouble, and though they tried for weeks, they couldn't save him. He slipped into a coma and died shortly before his fiftieth birthday. Not long after, on the anniversary of our ordination, his widow, Kathleen, posted an essay on Facebook that he had written for one of our classes.

Jim wrote about visiting Colorado to teach a course on law enforcement. He got there early and decided to take a drive. It was spring, and the snow was melting and the rivers were rising. At one point, he drove through a tunnel cut into the mountains and came out the other side to see something stunning: the most spectacular Rocky Mountain scenery. It gleamed with greatness, and Jim wrote that he felt he was encountering, more profoundly than ever, the presence of God. He realized that only the divine Creator could have created such staggering beauty. I think that may have been the beginning of his vocation. For the rest of his life, he talked about revisiting that corner of Colorado. That place, Jim wrote, was where he truly found God and discovered how close God remains to us.

Well, the fact is: God *wants* to be found. And he gives us so many opportunities—so many times when we travel through even the darkest tunnels of our lives and then come out the other side to find, unexpectedly, something surprising and beautiful, a glimpse of the Almighty.

It might be in a mountain. Or it might be in the next cubicle at work. It might be in watching a toddler learning to walk or in hearing a kind word from a stranger on a crowded subway platform.

It might be in something as small and seemingly insignificant as a broken piece of bread.

God delights in being with us.

As an old saying puts it: "Bidden or not bidden, God is present." He is here. He is close to us—walking with us, weeping with us, watching with us, rejoicing with us. He is here, amazing us.

We just need to look.

He wants to be found. Really.

And in finding him, whether on the altar or in a stunning piece of natural wonder, we find opportunities to love him, to adore him, to feel awe, to be humbled anew by his ceaseless love for us.

Years ago, a nun told me a story about a priest who was getting ready for Mass and filling a ciborium with unconsecrated hosts. Several tumbled out of the box onto the floor. He bent down to pick them up and toss them in the trash. But first, he held one between his thumb and forefinger and said, "Oh, to think what you could have become."

I often remember that and think of it whenever I find myself having to ready a ciborium before Mass. *Think of what this will become.*

By extension, in receiving the Eucharist, each of us can become a living ciborium, a living tabernacle. Think of what we can become.

It's one more reason to be all we can be.

CONSIDER THIS

Out of the darkness of my life, so much frustrated, I put before you the one great thing to love on earth: the Blessed Sacrament. . . . There you will find romance, glory, honour, fidelity, and the true way of all your loves upon earth.

— J. R. R. Tolkien[4]

It has been my custom, almost every Thursday evening, to attend Eucharistic Adoration at my parish. Rushing there after work made it almost impossible for me to spend a full hour or even a half hour with Our Lord, but I always looked forward to and cherished my weekly visits with him. In silence, I would share with him the innermost secrets of my heart and soul. Sometimes I would offer prayers of petition; other times I would offer prayers of thanksgiving. But quite often, I would just sit and quietly and peacefully enjoy the silent company of my ever faithful and changeless Friend.

—Regina Judith Faighes, Forest Hills, New York

TRY THIS

Even just a few minutes of Eucharistic Adoration can be transformative. Fulton Sheen used to say he composed his homilies before the Blessed Sacrament. I'm no Archbishop Sheen—who is?—but I have found that simply being present before the monstrance can clear my head and focus my heart; I always leave feeling better, and I think my own writing and preaching benefit as a result. If you can, carve out a little bit of time at a local church to just sit, look, and listen. What is God trying to say to you? What do you need to say to him? He's eager to hear what is on your mind. Try it sometime.

Too busy? Seek him elsewhere. In fact, seek him *everywhere*. The Jesuits encourage a spirituality rooted in the teachings of St. Ignatius of Loyola that seeks God in all things. Pray at the beginning of every day: *Dear God, help me to find you*. And then conclude each evening with: *Where did I find God this day? How was he present to me? How was I present to him? Did I tell him today, "My God, thank you. For everything. I love you"?*

PRAY THIS

Almighty and ever-living, ever-loving God,
teach me how to seek you in unexpected places;
to discover you when you are hidden;
to trust in you when you seem missing;
to recognize you when you come to me
in the face of a stranger,
the touch of a friend,
the voice of a child;
to notice your generous gifts;
and to thank you when I might otherwise take you for granted.
God, while I do not say it often enough, I say it now:
I love you. I adore you. I need you.
Thank you for your patience and your presence.
Even when I do not realize you are there,
I *believe* that you are.
I just do.
I need to remember that more and to doubt less
and to always be grateful for what you give me,
even when it is hiding in plain sight.
Thank you.
Amen.

CHAPTER 3

WHEN GOD TALKS

My sheep hear my voice; I know them,
and they follow me.
—John 10:27

God has a way of speaking to us, even when we aren't listening—or when we think we're too busy to pay attention. Often he is speaking when we don't even realize it.

I offer myself as Exhibit A.

People frequently ask me, "How did a writer and producer at CBS News end up becoming a deacon?" (CBS, after all, isn't exactly known as the "farm team" for Catholic clergy.) The roots of any vocation can be complicated and deep, but if I had to pinpoint the moment it all began for me, I'd have to single out one of the defining events of my generation: 9/11.

Many of us remember where we were on September 11, 2001. One of my most haunting memories, though, is the morning after.

I was working in New York City as a writer and producer for *60 Minutes II* at CBS News. The morning of the attacks, I was assigned to the newsroom to help write special reports. I spent all of the day, and into the night, watching the video of the towers falling again and again and again, as I pounded away at my computer, drank bad cafeteria coffee from a sty-rofoam cup, and tried not to think too hard about what had happened just a few miles from where I was sitting.

We finally signed off on our coverage at about 1 a.m. on September 12. It was impossible to get out of Manhattan—or to get in. Subways and trains had stopped. There were no cabs, no buses. CBS had booked a block of hotel rooms for us across town. So a group of us started the walk from West 57th Street and 10th Avenue over to Sixth Avenue in midtown.

The city was absolutely deserted. Traffic lights were blink-ing. But you couldn't miss this: every street corner had a soldier or a cop standing watch.

I remember crossing Broadway and looking down toward Times Square and being stunned. It was empty and dark. I actually stopped in my tracks. The government was so con-cerned about other attacks that—for the first time since World War II—every light, billboard, and marquee had been turned off. I kept on walking, finally checking into my hotel around 1:30 a.m. Everything was eerily quiet. New York, the city that never sleeps, may not have been asleep—but it was hold-ing its breath, closing its eyes, waiting for it all to change.

It was nearly 2:00 in the morning before my head hit the pillow. I awoke five hours later to the sound of sirens.

I looked out the window of my hotel. It was another spec-tacular September day, just like the one before. I could see the street below. Fire engines and ambulances were heading downtown. People were walking up and down the sidewalk. It seemed like just another day. I showered, threw on my clothes from the day before, and headed downstairs.

As I passed through the lobby to check out, I saw a man checking in: a fireman. He was still wearing his coat and boots. But they were barely visible.

He was covered, head to foot, in ash.

He looked like a ghost. As he signed in, some of the ash flaked to the floor.

I realized that what I had seen out my window had been an illusion. That was one view of the city. But this was the other one—shocking, disturbing, unbearably sad. It made the whole experience suddenly, tragically, inescapably real.

I walked back to the CBS Broadcast Center and began another day, but I was beginning it, really, in another world. Everything had changed. I was able to get home that night, and when my wife met me at the door, I hugged her for dear life.

For those of us in New York, the attacks of 9/11 lingered. They were there every day: in flags that suddenly appeared outside buildings; in candlelight vigils that occurred almost nightly; in the photocopied flyers that were taped to bus stops and lampposts all over the city, with grainy pictures from weddings or graduations, asking, *Have you seen her? Have you seen him?*

Miles from Ground Zero, near my apartment in Queens, you could even smell it. The cloud that had hovered over the site for days eventually drifted east. I remember standing on a corner near Queens Boulevard, waiting for a traffic light, and turning to another pedestrian. "Can you smell that?" I asked. She nodded. "It's from Ground Zero," she said. "Everybody's noticing it."

As days ticked by and the stories on the news became relentless, my own work in the news seemed less and less important. I realized with a blinding clarity that at the tender age of forty-two, my life had suddenly shifted. My goals seemed unimportant, superficial, small. What did any of it mean if it could all be gone in a matter of seconds? Was there something else I was supposed to be doing with my life?

In my questioning, I found myself circling back to something that had been an overlooked corner of my life—my faith. I was always the kind of Catholic who went to Mass, said his prayers, did what he was supposed to do. But that was about it. Now that changed. I found myself going out of my way to visit churches, lighting candles, whispering prayers. I picked up a book my father-in-law had given me several years earlier, one of his favorites from college: *The Seven Storey Mountain* by Thomas Merton.

And with that, a lot started to make sense. The book—chronicling a young Merton's journey from jazz clubs in New York to college to Catholicism and, ultimately, to a monastery in Kentucky—struck a chord. To Merton, faith gave sense to what had been senseless—a shape to a life that had been shapeless. I decided I wanted to go on a retreat to a Trappist monastery.

To make a short story long, through a complicated series of coincidences and happy accidents, I ended up becoming a frequent visitor to Our Lady of the Holy Spirit monastery in Conyers, Georgia, outside Atlanta. And there, on an unremarkable Sunday, I heard a deacon preach for the first time.

He was from England, and he preached a homily about "the way, the truth and the life." I was mesmerized. My chest tightened. My throat felt dry. Something just clicked. "That could be me," I thought.

Wait. What? Where did that idea come from?

I spoke with the deacon after Mass and learned that he worked as a freelance producer for the BBC. Not only that, but it turns out our paths had crossed in surprising ways, and we both knew some of the same people in the CBS News London Bureau.

Was God pulling my leg?

No. He was sending a message. And for the first time in my life, I was listening.

And I kept on listening. Five years later, there I was, in a place I never expected to be, lying face down on the floor of a basilica, as a choir chanted the Litany of the Saints. I was being ordained a deacon.

The moral of this story: God very often has something to say to us—something surprising and profound and hilarious and inexplicably personal. But are we ready to hear it? Are our ears attuned? Are we open to what he may be trying to tell us? What began for me amid the horror of 9/11 became, with promptings and encouragements and quiet whispers and insane coincidences, something wondrous. It took a tug of the heart and, ultimately, a leap of faith. But it happened. All I needed to do was listen. And respond.

In the story of my vocation, I am continually amazed that God took the time to work on me and pull me in that direction—and, perhaps, I am even more amazed that I went where he was leading me.

But this too is part of how we let God know that we love him. When he calls, we answer. We keep ourselves ready for astonishment. We open our hearts to a mystery and let him take the lead.

We shut up and let him tell us what's on his mind.

Or, as they like to say in the recovery movement, we "let go and let God."

If we do that enough, fueled by faith and powered by prayer, it can help us do what I was talking about at the very beginning.

It can help us to be more than we are—and be all that we can be.

CONSIDER THIS

The essential thing is not what we say but what God says to us and through us. In that silence, He will listen to us; there He will speak to our soul, and there we will hear His voice.

—St. Teresa of Calcutta[5]

They say that people come into your life for a reason—sometimes for only a short time, and at other times, they play a huge part in your story, or you in theirs.

I was an only child, and my dad and I were very close throughout my life. When he passed away in 2004, that was a major thing for me. At the time, I was vocation director for our diocese, and our newly appointed bishop asked me to become pastor of a parish that was going to be building a new church. My dad had just passed away three weeks before. I was honored to be asked, but the bishop didn't really know me, and I understood that he simply needed to find someone to go to that parish.

I told him twice that I didn't think so, and each time, the bishop said, "Think about it. Pray about it"—the proverbial kiss of death! I didn't think it was the right time for me—but then, the second time I said no, *I got it!* Well, I got two things—one was that it seemed "no" was not the right answer for the bishop. But then I really got it: just maybe, God was using the bishop and his need to help me rather than burden me—to help me to cope and to give me a new direction and purpose for my life after my dad's death.

As I reflect later—that yes to the bishop might just have saved me.

So it's been about eleven years since we built the church, and I have spent more than fifteen of my sixty-two years of life as pastor of Our Lady of the Blessed Sacrament in Westfield, Massachusetts. Though it has not been an easy assignment—and, by the way, if someone asks you to build a church, run as fast as you can—this parish has become my home, and its people, my family. What a grace God gave me, disguised as a burden! I will be eternally grateful.

—Fr. Daniel Pacholec, Springfield, Massachusetts

TRY THIS

It can never hurt to ask yourself, "Is God trying to tell me something?"

Sometimes the path of life is strewn with bread crumbs, and God is encouraging us to follow them to see where they lead. People are put into our lives, choices are placed before us, and opportunities are offered that we never imagined. In my own life, I look back and see the events of the last fifty years as a series of dominoes, one falling after the other, finally pushing me to where I am now, serving as a deacon in New York City. It seemed random. But maybe not.

Looking back on your life, do you see a pattern? Do you sense God has pushed you in a particular direction? Prepare to be amazed. And prepare, as well, to offer prayers of gratitude. Give thanks to the Lord for creating this life for you and setting you on your way. What else does he have planned? And how can we be all we can be to help carry out that plan?

PRAY THIS

Heavenly Father,
I am nothing without you.
Teach me to be more by being open to you.
Open my heart, to hear your word.
Open my eyes, to see your generosity.
Open my ears, to listen for your promptings.
Open my mouth, to proclaim your praise.
Open my arms, to embrace those in need.
Make me always willing and able to let you into my life,
into my heart, into my being,
so that with you, I will be complete.
Thank you for making the impossible possible
and for giving me what you know I need.
Amen.

CHAPTER 4

I WANT TO BE IN THAT NUMBER

Strive for peace with everyone, and for that holiness
without which no one will see the Lord.
—Hebrews 12:14

In the last chapter, I talked about how my searching and praying eventually led me to read Thomas Merton's autobiography, *The Seven Storey Mountain*. One of my favorite stories from that book describes a kind of epiphany he had while walking the streets of New York with a friend. (Merton was always having epiphanies of one kind or another, and he never let any thought go unexpressed. His output as a writer was more than prolific; it was epic.)

Shortly after he converted to Catholicism in the late 1930s, Merton was walking the streets of the city with his friend Robert Lax. Lax was Jewish, and he asked Merton what he wanted to be now that he was Catholic.

"I don't know," Merton replied, adding simply that he wanted to be a good Catholic.

Lax stopped him in his tracks.

"What you should say," he told him, "is that you want to be a saint!"

Merton was dumbfounded.

"How do you expect me to become a saint?" he asked Lax.

Lax said, "All that is necessary to be a saint is to want to be one. Don't you believe that God will make you what he created you to be if you will consent to let him do it? All you have to do is desire it."

Thomas Merton knew his friend was right. Merton, of course, would go on to become one of the great spiritual thinkers and writers of the last century. His friend Bob Lax would later convert to Catholicism himself—and begin his own journey to try to become a saint.

The words Lax spoke ring down through the decades to all of us today. Because they speak so simply and profoundly to our calling as Catholic Christians: to become saints, out of love for God, and to spend our lives trying to achieve that goal.

Of course, if you only want to be a run-of-the-mill Christian, that's probably all you'll ever be. Everyone can do just enough to get by. It's not hard to be average.

But the message Christ sends to all of us is an invitation to be something more.

I'll say it again: be all that you can be.

Be a saint.

If anyone has any doubts about how to do that, every year in the liturgy on All Saints Day, the Church offers us a handy guide—a famous passage from St. Matthew's Gospel. You might call it "Becoming a Saint for Dummies."

We know it better as the Beatitudes.

"Blessed are." With those two words, Jesus begins a beautiful instruction on how to live the life of a saint. Pope Benedict XVI has taken that a step further: in his remarkable book *Jesus of Nazareth*, he suggests that the Beatitudes are nothing less than a self-portrait of Christ.

As such, they should become our own self-portrait: to be poor in spirit, to be meek, to be merciful, to hunger and thirst for righteousness, to be clean of heart, and to make peace.

These are the traits of people who want to be saints.

Most of us are familiar with the phenomenal stories of the saints of the Church. We grew up hearing of how John was beheaded and how Stephen was stoned; how Francis received the stigmata or how Therese suffered humiliations and disease, dying an early death.

You hear stories like that, and you can't blame Thomas Merton for not really being eager to be a saint. The life of a saint is hard work—and pain and suffering are often part of the job description.

Remember Don Hewitt's philosophy? "Tell me a story." Beyond the sobering stories of the saints that we tend to hear, there are countless stories of saints—millions, throughout the centuries—that we don't hear.

These are the anonymous saints who go about their daily lives quietly, peacefully, joyfully, finally entering into the fullness of grace without doing anything more dramatic than merely living the Beatitudes.

They are the unsung saints.

If you visit the Cathedral of Our Lady of the Angels in Los Angeles, you'll see magnificent tapestries lining the walls, designed and executed by the artist John Nava. They are dramatic, realistic, and contemporary depictions of ordinary people of extraordinary character. And they adorn the walls of the cathedral the same way that stained glass windows once decorated the great Gothic cathedrals of Europe. (Los Angeles, being prone to earthquakes, isn't really conducive to big stained glass expressions of saintliness. But these tapestries fulfill that function beautifully with thread and paint.)

In the tapestries, you can see all the familiar saints, whose names we know, in a row facing toward the altar, as if in line for Communion. It is literally and figuratively the communion of the saints. There is St. Nicholas, St. Gregory, St. Thomas Aquinas, St. Francis, St. Clare . . . and on and on, with their names over their heads.

But scattered among those saints are people without names, people you won't find in *Butler's Lives of the Saints*. A teenage girl. A young man from the barrio. Children in contemporary clothes. It is a beautiful and eloquent depiction of the saints who walk among us, whose names we will never know.

These unknown saints, of course, are just as worthy of honor and recognition as the ones who are known. They look like us. They look like people we might pass on the street. If they can be holy, can't we all?

What does it take to join them?

As Bob Lax explained, all you really need is to want to be a saint.

God—our loving Creator, who wants us to be with him forever—will do the rest.

A famous anthem tells us: "When the saints go marching in, I want to be in that number." Well, who wouldn't? Who wouldn't want to march in step with those who lived the Gospel—caring for the sick, sheltering the homeless, clothing the naked, loving God and neighbor?

Do we want that? Do we want that *enough*?

Look at their lives, and you find a lesson plan for following Jesus. The saints, I think, have much to teach us—lessons in how to love, how to give, how to forgive, how to persevere, how to pray. They show us how to get up when we fall; how to serve with joy; how to keep our eyes fixed, not just on the cross of Good Friday, but on the empty tomb of Easter Sunday. The saints somehow managed to do that and help to point the way for us.

The communion of saints is just another gift from God.

And our desire to honor and imitate them can be our gift *to* God—a lived expression of our love for him that, just maybe, can point us on the path to paradise.

CONSIDER THIS

The Lord asks everything of us, and in return he offers us true life, the happiness for which we were created. He wants us to be saints and not to settle for a bland and mediocre existence. . . . Holiness is the most attractive face of the Church.

—Pope Francis[6]

About saints—I tend to like the more obscure ones, the ones the hagiographers haven't gotten ahold of and scrubbed free of all their wonderful faults.

One is St. John de Brébeuf, one of the North American martyrs: a refined French Jesuit who hated the hard life among the Iroquois, but when offered a chance to stay in France, he returned to them.

Then there is St. Camillus. In his younger days, he was something of a rounder: a mercenary, a gambler, and possessed by an incendiary temper. Once, after becoming Camillus the Hospitaller, he tossed an unscrupulous supplier of flour—and his wares—quite literally onto the street, thus incurring a hernia that plagued him the rest of his days. My kind of guy, given my own temper.

Last but not least is Martha. I can relate to any woman who feels comfortable telling God what to do and who has to be called by name, not once but twice, before stopping to listen. But I think that same bold friendship is what brought her to one of the great declarations of faith in the midst of heart-crushing grief.

I like my saints with warts. Because it's all too clear to me that if not for my own warts, I have little chance at holiness.

—Dr. Barbara Golder, Chattanooga, Tennessee

TRY THIS

Wanting to be a saint begins with knowing just what a saint is—and who filled the job requirements. Take a little time to read about them, learn about them, marvel at them. An easy place to start is with monthly devotionals—*The Word Among Us*, *Magnificat*, and *Give Us This Day* are easily available online and in print. They publish short biographies of saints and blesseds every month; you may be surprised at whom you meet and the lives they lived.

Beyond that, a great resource for any home library is *Butler's Lives of the Saints*, a handy compendium of holy lives well lived. Learn about your name saint and, for your profession or vocation, your patron saint. Pray with them regularly. Ask them for their intercession and help. And ask yourself, "What does this remarkable figure have to teach me? What does this life—a life that was, like mine, full of struggles and setbacks and disappointments and joys—illustrate about what it means to walk in the footsteps of Christ?" Meditating on the lives of the saints can go a long way toward helping us become like them.

PRAY THIS

O Lord of saints and sinners,
guide me in your way to help me become a saint!
Take my tattered soul, and stitch it back together.
Take my wounded heart, and help it heal.
Take my rough clay, and shape it into something smooth
and beautiful:
a soul seeking to serve you and love you
by serving and loving others.
Place into my life the people I need
to help me walk this path:
models of holiness and prayer, yet people of imperfection
who have also found their way to you.
You know the kinds of models I need—
guide me toward those who will teach me how to live,
how to love,
how to pray,
how to sacrifice,
how to surrender,
how to love you more completely,
how to follow you boldly with steadfast hope.
I ask this through your Son, Jesus Christ,
who came into this world for sinners like me.
Amen.

CHAPTER 5

LET THERE BE LIGHT

God looked at everything he had made,
and found it very good.
—Genesis 1:31

"Let there be light" (Genesis 1:3). It may be one of the best opening lines a character in an epic story could ever speak—and it's fitting that the character is God.

His first recorded words in all of Scripture literally set the stage for everything that will follow.

First, they tell us that he didn't intend for us to dwell in darkness. He meant for his creation to be a place where there was, first and foremost, *light*. What he was setting out to create would be something that was radiant. Luminous. Bright with possibility.

And that gives us the second important idea, which we easily neglect or overlook: God is a creator.

Scratch that. What I mean to say is that God is *the* Creator. An angel once reminded a questioning young girl that "nothing will be impossible for God" (Luke 1:37). Put another way, *everything* is possible with him.

Like any artist throughout history, at the beginning of time, God needed light so he could see what he had to work with;

he was setting out to craft, shape, mold, imagine, build. And what he was doing was nothing less than the definitive act of creation: he was summoning up something—everything!—out of nothing.

How did it turn out?

Critics today may look around and quibble. But Genesis tells us that in the beginning, it was "very good" (1:31).

Really, it was. And it is.

Now, countless millennia later, we are continually uplifted and sometimes thunderstruck to realize that creation didn't end with Genesis. God's creation continues all around us—and, in fact, through us. The greatest of all artists has endowed us with the skills, talents, and temperaments to take the raw elements of the world—everything from mud and wood to our own heartbreak and joy—and continue to express the Creator's endless creativity with our own hands, eyes, voices, and minds.

Art is one of God's enduring and often surprising gifts. What a wonder it is! That is the power of art and the artist. Michelangelo's *David*, Van Gogh's *Starry Night*, Beethoven's symphonies, a Jessye Norman aria . . . the heart and the head can barely contain it all. (Not to mention the exquisite balance of color and light that a five-year-old captures with crayon and that is preserved in the permanent collection of the gallery on the family refrigerator. *That* is art!)

The art we give, and that is given to us, manages to connect us in a powerful way to the source of all art, affirming again and again with every trumpet blast and brushstroke that God just can't stop creating. And his ulti-mate creations, we mere mortals, make all that possible, despite our flat notes and botched colors, because "noth-ing will be impossible for . . ." Well, you know.

So what is a busy person to do with so much wonder to see, hear, and experience?

Whatever we do, first of all, we need to be amazed.

Not just tickled or impressed.

Amazed.

The simple fact that God has taken the time to create this creation and create creators to create *more* creation is . . . amazing.

My parents used to tell about an episode from our last big family vacation. I have no memory of this and have to take their word for it.

I was five years old, and we headed out West to visit places like Pike's Peak and Mount Rushmore. Along the way, we stopped overnight in, I think, St. Louis. A movie theater near our motel was showing *The Sound of Music*. My parents thought this would be a great night out, so they took my sister and me to see it. Before the movie started, my mother bought me a Hershey bar, figuring that would keep me enter-tained if the movie didn't.

She should have saved her money.

Over two hours later, as the movie ended and the cred-its rolled, it was clear to my mother that I hadn't budged. The candy bar had melted all over my hand. I hadn't even tasted it; I'd just held onto it tightly for dear life. I was mes-merized by the movie—the scenery, the music, the singing,

Julie Andrews. The whole thing knocked my five-year-old self out. I was transfixed, completely transported to another world, one with yodeling and marionettes and nuns and Alps.

I don't intend to argue here whether *The Sound of Music* is great art. But I will say that God's creation can have that effect on us, all of us, and we should be grateful for every opportunity to feel overwhelmed by it—every chance to be awed to the point where the chocolate melts in our hands.

Many years after that experience, I found myself in another theater, the Metropolitan Opera House in New York, sitting in a box with a television reporter and his wife who had season tickets to the Met. He invited me as his guest one night, and we sat there for nearly four hours as Figaro sang his way through misadventures of love and, ultimately, marriage.

If I remember correctly, there were no Alps.

I woke up as the curtain came down on the first act.

My reporter friend sighed contentedly. "I love opera," he said proudly and gratefully. "I find it so transporting."

Recounting that experience later to another friend, I said, "That's the difference between him and me. When I want to be transported, I take the subway."

But each of us, however we can, need art and God's gift of art for that simple reason: we need it to take us somewhere.

If we want to help make our lives extraordinary, we ought to look for opportunities to experience that kind of amazement and joy—and thank God for it.

And then we need to repay him in the only way we can: with our lives.

Pope St. John Paul II, an artist himself—in his early life, he was a playwright, actor, and poet—wrote a Letter to Artists in 1999 that explained this beautifully:

"Not all are called to be artists in the specific sense of the term," he wrote. "Yet, as Genesis has it, all men and women are entrusted with the task of crafting their own life: in a certain sense, they are to make of it a work of art, a masterpiece."[7]

How is your masterpiece going?

CONSIDER THIS

God therefore called man into existence, committing to him the craftsman's task. Through his "artistic creativity" man appears more than ever "in the image of God," and he accomplishes this task above all in shaping the wondrous "material" of his own humanity and then exercising creative dominion over the universe which surrounds him. With loving regard, the divine Artist passes on to the human artist a spark of his own surpassing wisdom, calling him to share in his creative power. Obviously, this is a sharing which leaves intact the infinite distance between the Creator and the creature, as Cardinal Nicholas of Cusa made clear: "Creative art, which it is the soul's good fortune to entertain, is not to be identified with that essential art which is God himself, but is only a communication of it and a share in it."

That is why artists, the more conscious they are of their "gift," are led all the more to see themselves and the whole of creation with eyes able to contemplate and give thanks, and to raise to God a hymn of praise. This is the only way for them to come to a full understanding of themselves, their vocation and their mission.

—Pope St. John Paul II[8]

For as long as I can remember, I have found God in stories. From issues of faith and doubt in the TV series *Lost* to a metaphor for the communion of saints in *Star Wars: The Rise of Skywalker* to instances of the supernatural in Dean Koontz novels, popular culture often presents us with reflections on the divine if only we have the eyes to see them. And the great thing about stories is that they don't necessarily tell us what to believe, like a preacher in the pulpit, but rather they show us the results of believing and acting in a certain way, allowing us to internalize the moral and spiritual struggle and come to our own decisions.

In light of my affinity for stories, it's appropriate I wound up working for The Christophers, a media organization founded in 1945 by Fr. James Keller. Fr. Keller understood that the arts, media, and popular culture have the power to influence millions of people, so one of our ministries became the Christopher Awards, which honor books, movies, and TV programs that affirm the highest values of the human spirit. When we're exposed to stories that shine a light on our struggles, as well as on virtues like faith, courage, hope, and love, we're subtly nudged toward becoming better people. So the next time you watch or read a story, pay attention to see if you can find signs of the divine. God might be speaking to you in this unexpected way.

—Tony Rossi, Queens, New York

TRY THIS

Let's just admit it. Everybody is a critic.

Does anybody not have an opinion about books, movies, TV shows, hairstyles?

Listen to any conversation in a bar, pizza parlor, or local diner after a late showing of a movie has let out on a Saturday night. Or hear the debate in any living room after spending a couple of hours with friends watching Netflix.

But how often do we ask ourselves, after watching a movie or listening to an album or reading a book, "What is God revealing here? What is he trying to tell me, others, the world?" It may not be deep; it may not be profound. But if something affects us, moves us, or challenges us, there is something (or Someone) at work. The fact is, so much of what we see in our created world came from human hands and our limited imagination and skills—but behind much of it was another Creator. Are we able to set aside our cynicism, our criticism, and see that?

Do we appreciate that?

If nothing else, we should cultivate a sense of appreciation, even thankfulness, for the creative impulse behind every work of art—even if we can't stand it. It came, after all, from one of us, another of God's creatures. Try to see the world around us, and all the created things within it, as God continuing his "very good" creation in a thrilling, baffling, sometimes infuriating, and delightfully unpredictable way.

To try and do that, I think, is to try and see the world, not through our eyes, but through God's.

It can serve as a prayer of thanksgiving, a living psalm of love, to the One who made it all possible. It can open our hearts and broaden our minds, helping each of us to realize just how varied God's palette really is.

It is also a way to appreciate even more this extraordinary life we have been given—and that has been given, of course, to others as well.

PRAY THIS

O God,
Creator, Artist, Builder, Dreamer,
grant me the grace to see in all creation
your signature.
Help me to recognize your work
not only in the world around me
but in the works of those continuing your creation.
Painters and sculptors, composers and writers,
men and women whose hands become your instruments,
shaping and imagining and fulfilling
all that you mean them to do.
Help me also to see, in those I meet,
beautiful examples of your creativity.
May I marvel at the work of your hands,
the ingenuity of your vision,

the breadth of your overwhelming talent:
my brothers and sisters in this world around me.
Finally, help me to fulfill my own artistic ambitions
and create of my own life
a thing of beauty, and faith, and priceless love.
Help me to make of it
a masterpiece.
I do it in your name, and for you,
with gratitude and joy.
Amen.

CHAPTER 6

THE GIFT THAT KEEPS ON GIVING

As they prayed, the place where they were gathered
shook, and they were all filled with the holy Spirit and
continued to speak the word of God with boldness.
—Acts 4:31

I'll make this confession right here at the start: I'm a Holy
Spirit fanboy.

As I mentioned earlier, the deepest stirrings of my own vocation began at the Monastery of the Holy Spirit in Conyers, Georgia—I'm convinced that's no coincidence—and throughout my ministry, in times of struggle or hardship or aridity, the Spirit has inevitably come to my aid. The promptings have been real and sometimes not very subtle, and they have always left me dumbstruck.

Stumped for a homily idea? Scared into silence about what to tell someone struggling with a spiritual problem? Worried about the road ahead? The Holy Spirit has always been there to rescue me, in one way or another.

So when I think of how God has shown his love for us and how he continues to express it in ways large and small, I can't help but think of the Spirit.

Let's consider, for just a minute, Pentecost: the birthday of the Church.

It's different from most big feasts in the Church. We don't hang lights or exchange gifts. We don't wear fancy hats or eat lots of candy. There are no big Pentecost sales at Macy's.

But maybe there should be.

I don't think we give this event the credit or attention it deserves. Part of that may be because the One who dwells at the center of this great feast, the Holy Spirit, is surprisingly low-key. Despite arriving with a roaring of wind and tongues of fire, the Spirit is very much Someone who likes to stay in the background. He works behind the scenes.

To many of us, the Holy Spirit seems to be the quietest member of the Trinity. After all, in Sacred Scripture, the Father speaks often, and so does Jesus. But you'd be hard-pressed to find famous quotes from the Holy Spirit. It sometimes seems as if the Spirit is the Trinity's silent partner.

But I'd like to suggest that, in fact, the Spirit does speak. Eloquently. Passionately. Fearlessly.

Consider the Acts of the Apostles and the account of Pentecost: "They were all filled with the holy Spirit and began to speak in different tongues, as the Spirit enabled them to proclaim" (Acts 2:4).

Moments after his descent, the Spirit gave the disciples a voice, one that could not be contained in that upper room. Despite the wide range of cultures and languages gathered in Jerusalem that day, everyone present heard and understood. Someone even exclaimed, incredulously, "We hear them speaking in our own tongues of the mighty acts of God" (Acts 2:11).

Those "mighty acts" transcend time, place, language, culture. God's work is infinite. It is "catholic" in the truest sense of what that word means: it is universal.

It is limitless. And it is timeless.

Look around you and know this: Pentecost never stopped.

It is still going on, here and now, wherever you may be.

And every one of us is a part of it.

Pentecost is the parent bringing a newborn child to be baptized—bending over that font to see that first splash of water on the head of a child and hear the first astonished cry from a brand-new Christian.

Pentecost is the teenager approaching the bishop to have her head marked with oil—feeling the sense of pride and gratitude that comes with being confirmed, fully initiated in the Catholic Church.

But that is only the beginning.

Pentecost is the sister in Iraq spreading the faith to school children whose lives may have begun in a world of terror and war but who are standing up to embrace the Prince of Peace.

Pentecost is the lay catechist in Ethiopia helping adults learn the Gospel and memorize the *Catechism*.

Pentecost is Mother Teresa bathing a beggar, Fr. Damien giving Communion to lepers, Maximilian Kolbe stepping forward for a husband and father and saying, "Take me instead."

It is Fr. Ignatius Maternowski, who volunteered to parachute into France on D-Day. While working to set up a hospital to treat the wounded of both sides, he was shot and killed by a German sniper—the only Catholic chaplain to die on D-Day.

Pentecost is the men who walked across a beach in Libya in orange jumpsuits and who knelt to give their lives because they refused to deny their faith in Jesus Christ.

Pentecost is all those who are expressing faith, hope, and love in the face of persecution, martyrdom, and war—and doing it today just as they did 2,000 years ago.

Pentecost is more than just courage or defiance. It is hope. Resounding, tireless hope.

It is the tens of thousands around the world who enter the Church at Easter, seeing beyond the scandals and betrayals of our own age to glimpse instead something miraculous and beautiful—the grace of God.

Our tradition tells us that Pentecost began fifty days after Easter. But nowhere in Scripture does it say it ever ended.

It goes on.

It goes on every time someone leaves the confessional with their sins forgiven, full of grace and mercy and the desire to begin again.

It goes on every time a patient in hospice is anointed.

It goes on every time we leave church carrying within ourselves the Body of Christ—*becoming* the body of Christ—to transmit the Gospel in the world, "glorifying the Lord with our lives."

Pentecost can't be stopped.

We Christians have been around for 2,000 years. But know this: the Holy Spirit is just getting started.

I think of that great hymn of Pentecost: *Come Holy Ghost, creator blest, and in our hearts take up thy rest.*

Despite our problems, our weaknesses, our broken parts, and our sinful history, the Spirit continues to "take up thy rest" within each of us. He raises up popes and saints, missionaries and martyrs—countless witnesses to God's goodness in the world, a great cloud of witnesses that includes, incredibly, each of us.

When we are speechless, he helps us find the words. When we are frightened, he helps us find the nerve.

Make no mistake: the Holy Spirit is one of the gifts of God that just keeps on giving.

Once we realize that and accept that, what can we do with that?

The first thing I'd suggest is: give credit where credit is due. More often than not, we owe our deepest stirrings of faith, the most eloquent ideas, the most impulsive and creative missionary endeavors to the quiet but persistent work of the Holy Spirit.

The second thing: listen. Is something pawing at your conscience? Stirring your emotions? Planting wild and ambitious ideas in your head? It just might be the Spirit. Pray over it. Pray about it. And pray to the Holy Spirit for advice, counsel, direction. A woman I know likes to talk about how "the sneaky Spirit" works on her when she least expects it. Yeah, that's about right. The Spirit often digs holes and plants seeds in the middle of the night so that they blossom unexpectedly in the light of day. Know that. Embrace that. *Love* that. It is a sign of God's love for us.

Finally: pray. Pray to be vulnerable. Pray to be open to the promptings of the Spirit—and carve out time every day to actually pray to this member of the Trinity. Pray to shut up and listen when God is trying to tell you something—because, very often, he won't send a message by text or Twitter. He'll use the Holy Spirit. (That tweeting you hear may be from a bird, but not the one you think . . .)

I could go on. (I'm a fanboy, after all.) But you get my drift. God sent the Spirit at Pentecost to keep an eye on us, to keep us busy, and to help make our ordinary lives something extraordinary.

How could we refuse a gift like that?

CONSIDER THIS

A noble and delicate soul, even the most simple, but one of delicate sensibilities, sees God in everything, finds Him everywhere, and knows how to find Him in even the most hidden things. It finds all things important, it highly appreciates all things, it thanks God for all things, it draws profit for the soul from all things, and it gives all glory to God. It places its trust in God and is not confused when the time of ordeals comes. It knows that God is always the best of Fathers and makes little of human opinion. It follows faithfully the faintest breath of the Holy Spirit; it rejoices in this Spiritual Guest.

—St. Faustina Kowalska[9]

There was a time when every bump in the road meant that there still remained time enough to aim higher, to go faster, to work smarter—all with just a little more concentrated effort. Apply yourself, they told me, and get back up after every fall. Regroup, retool, reboot, reset. Sound advice, that. And always—always—prepare yourself for the worst while keeping a fistful of fingers crossed for the best. That's been my go-to, my default, my defense. And it has served me well. Until now.

These days, I find that these resets often carry deeper, more unanticipated, more troubling costs. And every year that passes seems to strain the truth more than it does these dangerously decaying muscles. Routines and silence, once derided, are now highly prized mostly for their own sake and simplicity. I guess that this is more and more a function of age. Perhaps a growing desire for reconciliation. Or a core realignment with the One who has always loved me in spite of myself and through it all.

—Tom Zampino, New York City

TRY THIS

When was the last time you gave more than a passing thought to the Holy Spirit? If it's been a while, now is a good time to change that.

We bring the Holy Spirit into our spiritual lives every time we make the Sign of the Cross. And of course, we pay tribute to the Spirit at Pentecost and on the feast of the Most Holy Trinity. But praying to the Spirit at other times—really, every day—can cement our connection to this member of the Trinity and can help keep us aware and alert to his presence in our lives. Ask the Spirit to keep you always mindful of his gifts: wisdom, understanding, counsel, fortitude, piety, knowledge, and fear of the Lord. Pray for his accompaniment and support. Call on him in times of anxiety or worry (I have to do that a lot!). Beseech him to "enkindle in me the fire of your love."

The blazes of the first Pentecost are still burning, and the Holy Spirit is happy to fan the flames.

PRAY THIS

Come, Holy Spirit!
Keep the fires of faith burning within me and over me!
With you as my comfort, my guide, my inspiration, my counselor,
lead me on the right path,
walking the way of trust,
the way of courage,
the way of serenity,
the way of love.
May I always have faith that you are with me
and never lose hope.
For where hope abides, you abide too.
Amen.

CHAPTER 7

LORD, HAVE MERCY

Have mercy on me, God, in accord with your merciful love;
in your abundant compassion blot out my transgressions.
Thoroughly wash away my guilt; and from my sin
cleanse me.
—Psalm 51:3-4

One of my earliest memories involves what may be the most embarrassing moment of my young life.

I think I was seven or eight. My mother took me to St. Catherine Labouré parish in Wheaton, Maryland, not far from where we lived, for what was at that time a regular routine for Catholics on a Saturday afternoon. We were going to Confession.

We entered the quiet church, and I got in line and practiced saying the words just the way Sister Saint Margaret had taught us: "Bless me, Father, for I have sinned . . ."

I was kneeling behind a velvet curtain on a piece of cracked vinyl padding, pronouncing my young sins to a priest I couldn't see, hidden behind a screen and a cloth. I told him my sins, and he gave me my penance. I prayed the Act of Contrition—"Oh my God, I am heartily sorry for having offended thee"—then crossed myself, pulled aside the curtain, and went to the altar rail to kneel and pray.

The slate was clean! I could begin again.

After finishing the prayers, I returned to my mother's pew and went out into the parking lot. As she started the station wagon and backed out of her space, she had a word of advice. "Gregory," she said, "you've got to keep your voice down. I could hear you all over the church."

Well. That was pretty awful. I don't remember doing anything particularly *evil* at that age, but it was bad enough that I had to confess it and on that particular Saturday, it seems, the world knew it.

My ears turned crimson and I don't think they recovered until I entered college.

That may be one reason (among many) why I developed an aversion to Confession and spent a lot of my life avoiding it. But what I didn't realize then—and what many don't even grasp now—is that to avoid Confession, the Sacrament of Reconciliation, is to shun yet another loving gift from God.

It is a way to make things right when you feel they have gone wrong.

It is a way to dip your fingers into the font of grace.

It is turning over a new leaf—or, at least, turning over a clean page, to begin writing a fresh chapter in the ongoing love story between us and God.

An old saying affirms that "confession is good for the soul." I agree. But it is also a good way to express to God something we don't say enough: I'm sorry. Forgive me. I love you. Let's begin again.

It can be a difficult conversation to have. It can take some of us years to get up the nerve to even mouth the words.

Sometimes the conversation comes very late in life. But if you're lucky, it happens much sooner.

So it was with me. Many years ago, prompted by a lot of indecision and turmoil and difficulty in my own life, I did something I hadn't done in far too long. I found my way back to Confession. There I was, on another Saturday morning in yet another church, preparing to catalogue my sins yet again. It was time to begin writing on a clean page.

I went to St. Francis of Assisi parish in New York, run by the Franciscans in midtown Manhattan, a short walk from Penn Station. I went down into the basement and stood in line and nervously tabulated everything that had gone wrong in my life. The mistakes I'd made. The people I had hurt. The pain I had caused others. The pain I had caused God.

And when my turn came, I slipped into a small wooden room and sat across from a Franciscan friar in his brown robes. I looked down at the floor and saw his feet. He was wearing a pair of Nike sneakers. And all I could think of was that famous line from the Nike commercial: "Just do it."

And so I did.

"Bless me, Father, for I have sinned. It has been ten years since my last confession."

And before I could say anything else, he smiled and said, "Welcome back. It's good to see you again."

I'd never seen him before in my life. But I knew exactly what he meant.

With that, I began my confession. I spoke. He listened. He had heard it all before, umpteen times, from the quivering lips of countless pitiful sinners like me. When it was all over, he gave me a mild penance and some gentle advice. "Just live the Gospel," he said cheerfully. "Just live the Gospel."

He absolved my sins and ended by saying, "There you are. Good as new. God bless you."

God bless you. It was the first time in a long time that those words had stuck. They meant something. But beyond that: I knew I had been changed. I did feel, in fact "good as new." So I went back a few weeks later, and a few weeks after that—again and again and again. It became a habit.

In the years since, it has become a habit of hope, renewal, and peace—an opportunity for me to refocus my life and assess my priorities, an occasion for grace.

Who could ask for anything more?

In the busy tumult of life, celebrating the Sacrament of Reconciliation is celebrating every second chance that God, in his amazing generosity, continues to give every one of us. The door is always open; the light is always on. There is always another opportunity to make right what is wrong, to fix what is broken, to heal what is bruised or battered.

Here's the thing, busy person: it doesn't take long. A few minutes can wash away days or weeks or years of mistakes, misjudgments, bad choices, nasty habits. What takes longer, I think, is getting over what caused all those things in the first place. We are creatures of habit, and we fall easily into routines that aren't always productive, positive, or healthy. (Do you find yourself confessing the same sins again and again? Welcome to the club.) In her autobiography *The Long Loneliness*, Dorothy Day sums up succinctly what confession is about—and what sinning is about too:

"I have sinned. These are my sins." That is all you are supposed to tell; not the sins of others, or your own virtues, but only your ugly, gray, drab, monotonous sins.[10]

We aren't nearly as exciting or scandalous as we think.

But the point of all this isn't to shock the confessor; it is, quite simply, to make amends. The prayer of contrition that I learned over fifty years ago concludes the sacrament by putting the burden on us, as we address God who is "all-good and deserving of all my love" and vow "to do penance and to amend my life."

Whether we realize it or not, our lives are like the Constitution of the United States—they have amendments. Changes. Addendums. Revisions. And the point of reconciling ourselves to God is to get cracking and start putting them into action.

We do this for one singular purpose: so that we, the created, can be at peace once again with the Creator—and that enables us to give back to God the love he gives us.

CONSIDER THIS

The Sacrament of Penance or Confession is, in fact, like a "second baptism" that refers back always to the first to strengthen and renew it. In this sense, the day of our Baptism is the point of departure for this most beautiful journey, a journey towards God that lasts a lifetime, a journey of conversion that is continually sustained by the Sacrament of Penance. Think about this: when we go to confess our weaknesses, our sins, we go to ask the pardon of Jesus, but we also go to renew our Baptism through his forgiveness. And this is beautiful, it is like celebrating the day of Baptism in every Confession.

—Pope Francis[11]

In my forty-seven years as a priest, I've heard thousands of confessions: first confessions, last confessions, and the regular "It's been a month/year/decade since my last" confessions. There's something about the first confession of a second grader that often plays out in confessions made all through life, right up to the very end. First penitents are generally nervous and afraid. They either don't know what to expect, or they expect the priest to be surprised, upset, or scolding in reaction to their list of (very predictable) sins. Of course, if a confessor is graced by the awareness that he's sitting in for Jesus, then his response will be loving, gentle, compassionate, and friendly.

And so year after year, second-grade boys and girls leave the penance room considerably more at ease than when they entered it. They've been refreshed by an encounter with grace that they might not be able to put into words but that, in their young hearts, they know to be real.

Although our list of sins changes with the various temptations that life and aging hand us, many adults come to the sacrament (or stay away from it) because, not unlike when they were younger, they're not sure what to expect, or they expect the priest to be surprised, upset, and scolding in response to their confessed failings. While the grace of God is constant and consistent, human nature doesn't change much at all. Young, old, or in between, the Holy Spirit nudges our consciences, plants the seeds of contrition, and takes us by the hand to this sacrament of mercy. How curious that we are so often reticent to reach out for that grace that is so freely given and shared with us when we want to be at peace with God and ourselves.

Year after year, decade after decade, I see men and women leave the penance room considerably more at ease than when they entered it. They've been refreshed by an encounter with grace that they might not be able to put into words but that, in their hearts, they know to be pure sacrament: souls are cleansed, hearts unburdened, and consciences cleared. And all because Jesus loves, forgives, and welcomes us sinners home, into the embrace of his strong and saving arms.

—Fr. Austin Fleming, Concord, Massachusetts

TRY THIS

I think an important building block of the extraordinary life is a sincere and healthy sense of humility, including the desire to admit to the God who loves us that we have failed him and we want to do better because of our love for him. The best place to do that is your friendly local confessional. But a heartfelt daily examination of conscience can work wonders too—compelling us to look at how we've succeeded, how we've failed, and how we can do better, particularly when it comes to our relationship with God.

So while you're lying awake at night, staring at the ceiling and wondering if you forgot to turn off the iron, ask yourself:

What have I done to please God today? What have I done that disappointed him?

How have I expressed my gratitude and love for God?

How have I neglected him? My friends? My family? Others who might have needed me?

How can I do better tomorrow?

What can I do to be all that I can be?

PRAY THIS

Father of mercies,
thank you for the gift of your limitless love.
Guide me in the way of your mercy
to be as merciful to others as you are to me.
Help me to give, when I'd rather hold back.
To forgive, when I'd rather turn away.
To listen, when I'd rather ignore.
To understand, when I'd rather rebuke.
Help me to always remember
that by being merciful to others,
I can live out the mercy you have extended to me,
and express, even in a modest and imperfect way,
my love and gratitude for what you have done for me.
Amen.

PART TWO

HOW WE LOVE OUR NEIGHBOR

CHAPTER 8

ALL ARE WELCOME

Let mutual love continue. Do not neglect hospitality,
for through it some have unknowingly entertained angels.
—Hebrews 13:1-2

O n an ordinary and unremarkable Sunday back in the
early 1990s, my world began to change with just a simple tap on the shoulder.

I was standing in the back of a church in Astoria, Queens,
biding my time during the last Mass of the day. I remember
looking at my watch and wondering if I could make a break
for it after Communion. Then came the tap and the voice.

"Hey, pal," it said, "can you help take up the collection?"

I turned around and encountered a little man with greased-
back hair, brooding eyes, and breath that reeked of cigarettes
and Certs. He was clutching the long handle of a wicker collection basket. I shrugged. "Okay," I said. "Where do you
want me to go?" He pointed to a side of the church and told
me to wait for my cue. A moment later, we headed down the
center aisle to the front pew, genuflected, and started taking up the collection, working our way toward the rear (or
maybe front?) of the church, by the entrance.

And that was how my ministerial career began. With that, I became an usher—or, as we call it now, a minister of hospitality.

I don't remember being all that hospitable during my days as an usher; I mostly just waved the basket in front of people and watched grandmothers put in a twenty and take out a ten, or I saw parents coaching their preschool children in how to drop the envelope into the basket. "Just drop it, honey. You can let it go. Go ahead. Just. Let. It. Go. Give the nice man the envelope, dear. Please. *Now!*" And then the child would freeze, and one of the parents would end up doing it on their own.

But something that really stayed with me, vividly, was the fact that the people in the pews ran the gamut—different ages, sizes, colors, and backgrounds. James Joyce famously said of the Catholic Church, "Here comes everybody"—and working the aisles as an usher, you see that again and again.

Here are the people of God. For better or worse, in good times and in bad, here are the neighbors we are called to love: "Love your neighbor as yourself" (Matthew 22:39).

But just how are we supposed to do that? If that is the second of the two great commandments and if it is a cornerstone of an extraordinary life, how do we live that out?

I think it has to start with responding to that call, that tap on the shoulder, and offering what might be called Hospitality 101—a sense of acceptance and belonging and, yes, welcome. It may not involve rattling a basket and collecting money—for most of us, it doesn't—but it means seeing those around us as part of the same community, the same neighborhood, the same steadfast band of believers.

And it means seeing them with an attitude that says— to quote a hymn that people either love or hate—that "all are welcome."

The lyrics of that hymn, by Marty Haugen, exhort us to create a "house" in which everyone can live and love in safety.

I would submit that the house that the composer is imagining is more than a mere building, more than a church with walls and pews and collection baskets.

The house, really, is us. Every single one of us. It is the living Church, the body of Christ.

To be precise, the house we are building is nothing less than the human heart.

That great commandment, to love our neighbor as ourselves, calls us to make *ourselves* living centers of hospitality—vessels of outreach and acceptance, of compassion and concern. We are challenged to say to each of those we encounter, "You are welcome in this place, this heart that belongs to Christ."

It's a beautiful notion. But how often we fall short. We let our preconceptions, our pride, our own shortcomings get in the way.

A priest I know tells the story of making a trip to Europe shortly after he was ordained in the early 1970s. He was traveling by ship, which was the cheapest way for a young priest to travel back then, and he was heading to Rome to continue his studies. One morning, when he was sitting in the lounge, wearing his new clerical collar and writing postcards, an elderly woman stopped by his table. She looked haggard and weary, and a faded scarf was tied around her head.

Noticing his collar, she asked where he was from, and he told her, "New York." She asked him how he liked it.

"It's okay," he shrugged. "But dirty. A lot of garbage. A lot of bums."

She nodded sympathetically. "Well, remember, Father," she replied, "you never know when one of those bums might be Jesus."

He thought it was an odd thing for the old woman to be saying to a stranger. He tried to shrug it off. But it stuck with him.

A few days later, he arrived in Rome, and his class was invited to attend a Mass celebrated by Pope Paul VI in St. Peter's. During the liturgy, the pope went down to the congregation to give Communion to a few people—and one of those in line was the old woman the young priest had seen at sea. She was wearing the same dress, the same scarf.

The priest was floored. He turned to a friend. "That old woman with the scarf? She was on our ship. What is she doing getting Communion from the pope?"

His classmate looked at him, incredulous.

"You don't know?" he whispered back. "That's Dorothy Day."

The moral of the story? You never know when one of those bums might be Jesus—or when the stranger you bump into just might be a saint.

On the voyage of life, wherever it is taking us, we need to greet our fellow sojourners with generosity, with mercy, with love. We need to see them as part of God's handiwork—creations of the Creator—who are wondrously made. Do we do that? Do we even try?

We need to walk out into the world with a song of welcome in our hearts.

I think Jesus left Nazareth and ventured into Galilee that way. He was the ultimate minister of hospitality, and his heart was the ultimate "house" in which love made a home.

CONSIDER THIS

Let all guests who come be received as Christ would be, because He will say, *I was a stranger and ye took Me in.* . . . Let true humility be shown to all guests coming and going. By bowed head, or body prostrate on the ground, all shall adore Christ in them, Who, indeed, is received in their persons.

—The Rule of St. Benedict[12]

As an alumnus of Saint Meinrad Seminary in Indiana, I am a bit biased about Benedictine spirituality. I thank God that I was schooled in Benedictine hospitality there because it is a fundamental component of my life as a parish priest. I was ordained in June 2000 for my home diocese of Charlotte, but I have served all but one of those years at churches either in the Blue Ridge or the Great Smoky Mountains of western North Carolina. These churches vary in size, but they share the similarity of welcoming retirees, many of whom come on a seasonal basis, as well as tourists, especially in the summer and autumn. My present parish home in Brevard is a hub for many summer camps too.

People come here to be restored, whether for a long weekend, a week's vacation, or for a greater length of time. They seek closeness to God through receiving the sacraments and through taking walks or hikes or riding a bike through forest trails. I have heard confessions at my church and on the Appalachian Trail. Such seekers help me to avoid spiritual complacency. In return, I hope to offer them the assurance of Christ's peace. People come here for personal integration rather than for diversion. I hope and pray that I can help them not only to become more integrated but also to rejoice in sharing in eternal divine communion.

—Fr. Shawn M. O'Neal, Charlotte, North Carolina

TRY THIS

Webster's tells us that the word "hospitality" comes from the Latin word *hospitalis*, meaning "of a guest." But the Christian notion of hospitality means more than just offering someone a seat at your table or a bed for the night. It means—like the word "hospital"—to give someone care. To tend to his or her needs. It means to be like Christ to them and to try to *see* Christ *in* them.

For just one day, head into the world and look for Jesus at the bus stop, at Starbucks, in the post office, or in the line at the bank. Seek him at the grocery store, waiting for the elevator, copying invoices at the office. Remember, you never know when one of those bums might be Jesus.

For just one day, make of your heart a house where love can dwell not just toward those you know or those you like or those you recognize in your office building's cafeteria. Try to hold in your heart this radical idea: "All are welcome in this place."

You'll be taking one more step toward living an extraordinary life!

PRAY THIS

Father of welcome,
you welcomed the world into being
and welcomed the first man and woman into Eden.
Give me a welcoming, hospitable spirit,
that I may open my arms,
open my eyes,
and open my heart.
Help me to see beyond division
and beyond differences,
to seek common ground
and common good.
May I learn to embrace others
who are seeking their way to you.
Help me to remember the joy of the father
who welcomed home the prodigal son

and the patient persistence of the Good Shepherd
who never let one of his own be lost.
I pray to be generous in inviting others to know you—
as generous and giving as your Son!—
and ask that at the end of my days,
I will be welcomed home by you.
Amen.

CHAPTER 9

ATTENTION MUST BE PAID

Give to everyone who asks of you, and from the one who
takes what is yours do not demand it back.
Do to others as you would have them do to you.
—Luke 6:30-31

It sounds obvious, but it's something we easily forget: one
of the most constructive ways to love your neighbor as
yourself is to simply pay attention. Our neighbors deserve
that much.

Notice them. Listen to them. Look them in the eye. Be *present*
to them. Give them the gift of your time—and, by extension,
honor them. Whether we realize it or not, these are ways to
bestow on someone a sense of dignity, to give due respect to
one of God's children—and, you know, God loves things like
that. Jesus was good at this (more on that in a moment), and
holy men and women seem to be able to do it naturally.

Years ago, I read the following story about Archbishop
Fulton Sheen, recounted by his niece, Joan Sheen Cunning-
ham. It has always stayed with me.

In an interview, she explained what it was like to walk
through the streets of New York City with the most famous
priest in America. As she put it,

People would stop him all the time. They'd want to shake his hand. He'd always take an interest in whoever walked up, taking the time to greet them. He always welcomed them, and was never short with anyone. He was just my uncle back then, it didn't dawn on me until later that he was a celebrity.

Since he was known for his generosity, people would often come up to ask him for money, telling him how they were down on their luck. He'd hand them $20. I'd ask him, "How do you know that they're not putting you on; that they really need help?"

He'd answer, "I can't take the chance."

He had a great love for the poor. . . .When he was made bishop of Rochester, he would regularly go to the homes of poor people to celebrate Mass. . . .

He was also kind to outcasts. I remember one man that was disfigured by leprosy who always came to his radio broadcasts. People in the audience would see the man, cringe at his appearance and move away from him. My uncle would say to me, "Joan, go over and talk to that man, he's very nice."[13]

I wonder sometimes whether we have lost the ability to notice one another—not just someone in need or someone who has been outcast, but even members of our own circle, including our own family. When did we stop paying attention? Conversations in general have been reduced to texts on a phone. Dinner has become an opportunity for texting between bites. I've heard of families who make members put their phones in a basket on the table.

Years ago, when I first moved to New York City, I would take the subway to work and marvel at the people I'd see artfully folding pages of the *New York Times* into quarters, to make it easier to read in the crowded trains. It was urban origami. Now that's a lost art. We all have phones or tablets. It's also rare these days to see anyone looking at anything other than the device in our hands.

And we're missing so much!

I think of someone who went out of his way to pay attention—and the attention was repaid. Zacchaeus was so short, he had to climb up a tree to get a good glimpse of Jesus. In return, Jesus did more than notice him; he invited himself into Zacchaeus' home.

Do we take the time to notice those who are usually overlooked? Do we remember to pray for those who are so often forgotten?

A couple of years ago, my sister sent me some old photographs she'd uncovered. They were from 1983—pictures of my parents during their last visit to my father's hometown, Taylor, Pennsylvania, outside Scranton. During the trip, they decided to stop by the local churchyard where many of my father's family are buried.

One of the photographs showed the grave of a woman whose story I had often heard but whose name I never knew until I saw it engraved in stone.

Maria Kandra.

From what I know of her, Maria came to this country as a young girl in the early 1900s from a village called Margecany in what was then Austria-Hungary. Today, it is in Slovakia. Maria settled with her family in Pennsylvania in the hardscrabble coal mining town of Taylor. She married a boy from her village, George Kandra. These were humble people; I don't think he even graduated from high school. He worked, like many of the immigrants in the town, in the mines and lived in a modest wooden row house with outdoor plumbing, the kind of place some people might call a shack. George and Maria soon had a young daughter, Mary.

But George and Maria's life together was over before it had barely begun.

In the days after her daughter was born, Maria suffered from postpartum sepsis. Medical care was scarce and often unreliable for so many of the poor at this time. She never recovered. Maria Kandra died at the age of twenty-three. She left behind her twenty-four-year-old husband and their infant daughter.

He ended up remarrying a short time later. George and his wife, another young girl from his homeland, went on to have four children together—and one of them was my father. The rest is history.

But in my family history, Maria Kandra is someone who has been largely forgotten. We have no photographs of her. There is no one to tell her story. But I am haunted by the memory of that young girl who came to a strange place to start a new life—a life that was far too brief but a life that, indirectly, has touched my own.

I think of Maria Kandra and think she's not that different from Zacchaeus—someone easily overlooked, but someone Jesus paid attention to anyway.

Know this: God pays attention to each of us. Shouldn't we do the same for others?

Shouldn't we give a look, an ear, a hand to hold, or a shoulder to lean on?

Shouldn't we be *present* to those who sometimes feel as if they themselves are *absent*?

This is love. And it can make life—for us and for others—extraordinary.

CONSIDER THIS

The deepest level of communication is not communication, but communion. It is wordless. It is beyond words, and it is beyond speech, and it is beyond concept. Not that we discover a new unity. We discover an older unity. My dear brothers, we are already one. But we imagine that we are not. And what we have to recover is our original unity. What we have to be is what we are.

—Thomas Merton[14]

My teenage daughters came home recently from a day out with their friends and delivered the news. "Your dad is lit," one of the friends had said. And they all agreed; I'm lit.

"He's the litest," chimed in one of them.

No longer slang for drunk, "lit," in young people's parlance, means exciting, excellent. I guess that dovetails with the fact that all of our children's friends also call us Mom and Dad, not Mr. and Mrs. Nadal. I don't know how exciting or excellent we actually are, but I know why they've bestowed the appellation.

We pay attention to them, as we do our own children, other family, and friends. They often comment on how grateful they are that we listen to them, talk with them, and take their lives seriously. That's not an accident. It's by design.

I made a decision that people would come first in my life—not because I thought the world needed me, but I saw how much I needed them. *I need* human interaction. I need to share the journey just as much as I need oxygen. We all do. It's how God created us.

To look into another's eyes; to read the emotion in those eyes, on their face; to hear the tone of voice; to share joys, sorrows, peaceful moments, and adventures; to share what gives life meaning, direction, and purpose. This is where fulfillment and contentment reside.

That can't be done in a text message, a Snapchat, a Tweet, or an email. People aren't items on our ever-lengthening to-do list.

Breaking bread with friends and family, cooking a meal for them, serving them, sharing our love and friendship are what makes life beautiful in our home. And with so many beautiful young people buzzing around and with friends our age, there's nonstop laughter. It allows us all to be liberated for a time from the technology that isolates and alienates, and in those encounters, it is no surprise how easily and often God and his love become the topics of conversation, how he uses those moments to bind us all together in love and friendship.

That's lit.

—Dr. Gerard Nadal, Staten Island, New York

TRY THIS

I know it's hard, but imagine going a full day without your cell phone.

No, I'm not kidding. Really.

Imagine living the way we were *meant* to live—watching the world, looking into the eyes of another, experiencing life beyond the boxy confines of that instrument you carry in your pocket.

Try it.

Try going through a day—okay, start with just an hour—not texting, emailing, or snapping photos for Instagram. Try seeing the world with your own eyes, not through the frame of a screen.

Believe it or not, not so very long ago, this is how everyone lived. Can we do it again? Can we give all our attention to one another and, in doing that, love one another? I think so. I hope so.

PRAY THIS

Attentive God,
your "eye is on the sparrow,"
and I ask you to keep an eye on me.
See that I see others:
that I do not miss the poor, the weak, the small.
See that I am attentive to others,
as you are attentive to everyone.
Help my heart to see more clearly,
more generously,
more lovingly.
May I never be distracted by my own self-interest,
but be interested, above all, in you and those you love.
Look before me, to keep me from falling.
Look behind me, to keep me from danger.
Look around me, to keep me always aware of your world
that you loved into being.
Amen.

CHAPTER 10

OWED TO JOY

When he set for the sea its limit,
so that the waters should not transgress his command;
When he fixed the foundations of earth,
then was I beside him as artisan;
I was his delight day by day,
playing before him all the while,
Playing over the whole of his earth,
having my delight with human beings.
—Proverbs 8:29-31

If we want to think seriously about loving our neighbor, maybe we need to be a little less serious about it.

Think for a moment about something that makes you sublimely happy. Maybe it was a knock-knock joke told by your grandson. Or maybe it was the way your wife smiled when you came home at the end of the day. Or maybe it was staying awake to watch your newborn baby sleeping in his crib.

Think about those moments in your life that have given you joy.

Because in those moments, you have touched something of the essence of God.

One of the great theologians from the fourteenth century, the Dominican priest Meister Eckhart, defined the Trinity this way:

When the Father laughs at the Son and the Son laughs back at the Father, that laughter gives pleasure, that pleasure gives joy, that joy gives love, and that is the Holy Spirit.[15]

That definition says it all—and it reminds us of something too easily forgotten in our faith.

And that something is, you guessed it, joy.

In Eckhart's vision, the element that binds the Trinity together—what sparks its existence, really—is something exuberant. It is love brought about by joy.

The novelist Leon Bloy understood that. "Joy," he wrote, "is the most infallible sign of the presence of God."[16] Where joy is, there also is God.

But for whatever reason, many of us don't give joy its due. We tend to face the Lord with grim faces and furrowed brows. Is that what he really wants? Scripture reminds us, again and again, that God takes delight in creation. We shouldn't be afraid to express that or share in it.

To share in that joy is to feel the nearness and excitement of God's love for us.

The saints help point the way. There was St. Lawrence—one of the great deacons of the Church—who, while being roasted to death on a grill, told his executioners, "Turn me over, I'm done on this side." There was St. Philip Neri, who hung a sign on his door that said, "The House of Christian

Mirth." And there was Padre Pio—a man, I suspect, that no one thinks of as being a comedian. In the 1960s, when the Red Brigade was sparking violence in Rome, people began carrying a picture of Padre Pio for protection. One day Padre Pio was going into Rome and a friend asked him, "Aren't you worried about the Red Brigade?" "No," he replied. "I have a picture of Padre Pio."

These saints understood the importance of a happy heart. They knew that it is part of what makes us human—but also what connects us to the divine. If joy is at the heart of God, it's also at the heart of *us*, for we are made in the image of God.

And you can find joy in the thousands of small miracles God places before you.

I remember well when I took part in my first wedding as a deacon—assisting at the Mass for my nephew just a few days after I was ordained. Twenty-one years earlier, he had been a ring bearer in my own wedding. And there I was, having the privilege of serving as the deacon at *his* wedding. Joy was there, overflowing. And so was love.

And so—inevitably—was God.

Joy and love are so closely entwined because it is impossible to love with an attitude of gloom or despair.

"A joyful heart," said Mother Teresa, "is the normal result of a heart burning with love."

She could be describing God's feelings for us—or even, perhaps, our feelings for one another.

Want to know what true joy is? Find the nearest child. Kids get it. They are consumed by wonder, fascination, delight.

When I was five years old, my mother took me to Wheaton Plaza shopping center in Wheaton, Maryland, to see Santa Claus. Any five-year-old will tell you: this is a very big deal. And it was even more so for me because I wanted a new two-wheel bike, with monkey bars and a banana seat. I was hoping to have a good talk with Santa about it.

But this particular year, I was coming to Santa Claus harboring a dark secret: I was a chronic thumb sucker. Nothing my parents could do would make me stop. They put hot mustard on my thumb. They put nail polish on it. They yelled at me. They scolded me. They cajoled me. They bribed me. Nothing worked.

But then came that visit to Santa. We stood shivering in the cold for several long minutes—this was in the days before enclosed shopping malls!—and then I was ushered into a tiny wooden structure decorated to look like a gingerbread house. I climbed onto Santa's knee to tell him what I wanted. He listened very politely to what I had to say and then replied, "Well, I'm going to try, but first you have to do something." He paused for dramatic effect. "Stop sucking your thumb."

I was stunned. How did he know?! Wow.

To make a long story short, when I climbed down from Santa's knee, I vowed to go cold turkey. According to my parents, that did it. I never sucked my thumb again. And Santa kept his part of the bargain: I got the bike of my dreams. It is one of the happiest Christmas memories of my childhood.

My mother never tired of telling that story—even when I was in college, to my endless irritation—but I look back on it now, and it only makes me smile. What is it about being so young and full of wonder that makes us so willing to believe, to hope, to dream?

I see it in my nieces and nephews at family gatherings: endless energy, raucous laughter, giddy delight in everyone and everything. Kids intrinsically know that life is hilarious, and if you aren't laughing along with it, what's the point?

Kids are able to tap into something we easily forget as we grow older: pure, unvarnished, uncensored joy. They just find it easier to be joyful. After all, when you're two or three, every day is amazing and overwhelming and new. (A two-year-old's monologue with self: "See my toes? Aren't they hilarious? Come on, they're a *riot*!")

Want to have an extraordinary life? It helps to make that life an ode to joy—and remember too how much we owe to joy. What makes you laugh out loud?

It's not just getting all the jokes or giggling foolishly at a bad one-liner or smiling when Santa brings you the gift you want. It's more than that. Years ago, I saw a t-shirt for sale at a street fair in New York that showed a stick figure walking down a road, smiling, and the caption read, "Enjoying the journey." Yeah. That's a big part of it. It's savoring what comes along, no matter where the road takes you, and appreciating that at least you're able to make the trip.

From a spiritual perspective, it's giving back to God some of what he has given to us when he offered us the gift of life. Can anyone doubt that the Lord looks on us with wonder and joy and even delight? (We'll skip over the frequent times he gazes at his children with displeasure and sorrow.) Approaching the world from a place of joy means savoring the abundant blessings we have been given. It's having a grateful heart. It's looking at creation and all that is in it with a sense of possibility and, yes, joy.

In my first job at CBS News, I was a production secretary. It was the least exciting job in the business and involved, more often than not, typing, answering the phone, and making airline reservations for globe-trotting producers. My tools included an enormous typewriter and a beige touch-tone phone. I also had a fax machine that connected me to our bureau at the White House and a ballpoint pen and yellow-lined notepad. That was about it. (It was a long time ago. When all else failed, we communicated with carrier pigeons and smoke signals.)

It wasn't exactly glamorous work, but it was thrilling to have a front row seat to history and to see the likes of Dan Rather, Walter Cronkite, and Charles Kuralt wander through the office and ask if they could borrow my phone to call London. And every day was a learning experience—how to craft a story, polish a script, book an interview, transcribe a press conference, and then crash on deadline and survive to talk about it.

The senior producer who hired me summed up his philosophy one evening at the end of a long and exhausting day. We slipped on our coats and walked out to M Street to head home. "Kid," he said, "the idea is to do it as long as you're having fun. When you stop having fun, it's time to get out of the business. Just have fun."

"Just have fun." Enjoy it—which means to take joy in. Take joy in what you do. Delight in it. Share that with others.

Because inevitably, you will be sharing something of God—imparting a sense of wonder and delight, laughter and hope.

And in giving that simple gift to another, we give as well a small taste of God's love.

CONSIDER THIS

An evangelizer must never look like someone who has just come back from a funeral! Let us recover and deepen our enthusiasm, that "delightful and comforting joy of evangelizing, even when it is in tears that we must sow. . . . And may the world of our time, which is searching, sometimes with anguish, sometimes with hope, be enabled to receive the good news not from evangelizers who are dejected, discouraged, impatient or anxious, but from ministers of the Gospel whose lives glow with fervour, who have first received the joy of Christ."

—Pope Francis[17]

I am aware not everyone is married to a comedian so I can't just give the advice "When something horrible happens, laugh about it!" but what I can stress, is the extreme importance of being open to laughing in the face of adversity and maintaining a sense of humor. Even if you are not the sick person but you visit someone in the hospital or are sick at home, bring joy with you!

Sometimes it seems everyone has been programmed to think that the appropriate way to enter the room when you visit a sick person is to have a sad, sympathetic look on your face and speak in a morose whisper. Yes, the patient is in pain and is going through something horrible, and we should empathize and have compassion, but that doesn't mean we have to come in like Debbie Downer. You would be amazed at what happens when people around you are filled with joy and positivity. Your breathing gets deeper, your blood pumps stronger. It actually strengthens your immune system when you smile and laugh. As my husband says, "Laughter is really the best medicine . . . after of course, you have real medicine."

—Jeannie Gaffigan[18]

TRY THIS

The surest way to cultivate joy—and spread it to others—is to remind yourself why you should be joyful in the first place.

And that begins with an attitude of gratitude.

So try this. Every evening, take a few minutes to count your blessings. Literally. Make a brief inventory of how you have been blessed—even if the only things that come to mind are the things that didn't go wrong. The check you didn't bounce. The virus you didn't catch. The test you didn't fail. And remember too the many small miracles of your life—friendships that enrich you, smiles that delight you. Give it to God with gratitude. And then vow to give that gratitude, and that small, quiet sense of joy, to someone else. Pay it forward. Pass it on.

PRAY THIS

Oh God of hope and joy,
guide me in the way of delight
to reflect your happiness to others.
Help me to remember your many gifts,
to be grateful for all your blessings,
and to become, in my daily life, one who brings those gifts
to those I meet.
Fill me with your light,
that I may shed light to others in darkness.
Grace me with your generosity,
that I may give to those in need.
Uplift my heart with your divine laughter,
that I may share joy with those who are sorrowing.
Make me an instrument of your joy
so I may one day share joy with you for all eternity.
Amen.

CHAPTER 11

HOW MAY I SERVE YOU?

You are the light of the world. A city set on a mountain cannot be hidden. Nor do they light a lamp and then put it under a bushel basket; it is set on a lampstand, where it gives light to all in the house. Just so, your light must shine before others, that they may see your good deeds and glorify your heavenly Father.
—Matthew 5:14-16

Pope Francis likes to talk about the idea of "encounter" and how important that is for Catholic Christians. As he said in his homily at Madison Square Garden in 2015, Jesus "urges [his disciples] to go out and meet others where they really are, not where we think they should be."[19]

It's a strikingly simple and straightforward idea, isn't it? But how often do we live it? How often do we spend our lives sighing, looking at the time, waiting for others to just snap out of it and be exactly the kinds of people we expect them to be? We run out of patience and, eventually, charity.

But that whole idea of encounter, of meeting people where they are, demands a certain amount of sacrifice and, I think, love. It says, "You're not here for me. I'm here for you. No matter who you are. Maybe I have something you need. How can I help?"

The result is fundamental to loving our neighbor. And loving our neighbor begins with recognizing just who our neighbor is. As Jesus reminded us in the parable of the Good Samaritan, our neighbors may not be who we think they are.

We might be shocked at what we find out about them.

And what we find out about ourselves.

Years ago, when I'd first moved to New York and was working at CBS, my wife asked me to stop by H&H Bagels in Manhattan on the way home from work. H&H was, by public acclamation and reputation, the best bagel shop in New York. Back in the day, H&H used to offer bagels on sale every afternoon, half price, after four o'clock.

So after work, I got a bag and went down to the subway station to head back to our apartment in Queens. The bagels were still warm. They smelled wonderful.

I went to get a fare card, and there was a homeless man standing by the window of the token booth. He was holding a cardboard cup, asking for money. I almost always avoid these guys, or ignore them, but this time I had an idea. Instead of giving him money, I asked him if he'd like a bagel. His face lit up. "Oh yeah!" he said, and he nodded. I reached into the bag and got one and handed it to him, and he just grinned and thanked me. He was overjoyed. You would have thought that I'd given him a sirloin steak.

I was feeling very proud of myself and my generosity. I felt so unbelievably holy and Christian. I went through the turnstiles and waited on the platform. My train came and as I stood there waiting to get on, I looked for my home-less guy. (Suddenly, he had become *my* homeless guy. I had taken a vested interest in him.) I couldn't see him. But then I noticed: he'd walked all the way to the end of the platform. And there, I saw, was another old homeless man, sitting on the ground.

My homeless guy took the bagel I had given him and broke it in two. He gave half to his friend.

My train came. I got on. And I watched them eating the bagel as we pulled out of the station.

And I was overwhelmed, almost to the point of tears.

I had thought myself so generous and so thoughtful. And yet a man who had next to nothing had given half of all he had to a man who had even less.

Besides being a lesson in humility, and generosity—showing me, very graphically, what it means to "love thy neighbor"—that moment was also profoundly Eucharistic. It was Emmaus in a subway station. I saw something of Jesus there, in that moment, in the breaking of the bread. I'll never forget it.

It was a valuable lesson to me in so many ways—but an important part is this: very often we are put into other peo-ple's lives, not for their benefit, . . . but for ours.

We not only meet them where they are, but they meet us where *we* are.

That is encounter.

And it can be a source of grace.

Encountering others, serving others, or *helping* others doesn't have to mean just keeping an eye out for anyone poor or discarded or needy or hungry—though, as the Gospels tell us, that's fundamental to the Christian way. No: caring about others and being open to encountering them can also mean simply lending a hand or an ear or a moment of attention. It's helping to bear a burden or carry a load; it's the neighbor helping move a sofa or a parent helping review homework or a brother showing a young sibling how to shoot a basket or play a good offense on a schoolyard basketball court.

It's offering a precious gift of time—the most precious gift any of us can offer, really—and saying, "Here. Take some of this. It's free."

And believe it or not, something that simple and generous can become an act of love. It's not just about showing love for another but about God conveying his love to every one of us—through us.

That encounter I had in the subway with a homeless man burned into my conscience and, in time, propelled me toward my vocation in the diaconate, a vocation whose very hallmark is service. Coincidence? I don't think so.

And I have to say, that vocation has made my life more than I ever imagined. I might even say it's been extraordinary.

CONSIDER THIS

The Gospels tell us how many people came up to Jesus to ask: "Master, what must we do?" The first thing that Jesus does in response is to propose, to encourage, to motivate. He keeps telling his disciples to go, to go out. He urges them to go out and meet others where they really are, not where we think they should be. Go out, again and again, go out without fear, go out without hesitation. Go out and proclaim this joy which is for all the people. . . .

Go out and proclaim, go out and show that God is in your midst as a merciful Father who himself goes out, morning and evening, to see if his son has returned home and, as soon as he sees him coming, runs out to embrace him. . . . An embrace which wants to take up, purify and elevate the dignity of his children.

—Pope Francis[20]

"Every time Mary said yes *to* God, she said yes *for* us." I have shared this statement many times, including in homilies I have presented. One might expect that this very simple yet profound statement came from a canonized saint, a theology professor, or a Church leader. But I heard these words from a man who never graduated from high school and is serving a lengthy prison sentence. He proclaimed these words when we were discussing the Annunciation during my very first visit to a state prison to lead a Bible study.

During deacon formation, the instructors repeatedly suggested becoming involved in prison ministry. I initially became involved in order to fulfill a requirement related to practical pastoral experience. I thought it would be temporary. Nearly a decade later, I still lead Bible studies several times a month at the same prison. The man who shared the profound statement about Mary still comes to the sessions. This outreach to those on the margins has turned out to be God's requirement for *me* to be fulfilled.

—Deacon Jim Hogomeier, Madison, Wisconsin

TRY THIS

Mother Teresa used to say that Jesus sometimes comes to us in the "distressing disguise of the poor." I would expand that statement even further. There are many ways of being poor. There are people who are lacking in love, in self-respect, in self-esteem. They know a poverty some of us can't imagine—spiritual, emotional, or intellectual. I think Jesus may sometimes come to us in the distressing disguise of the needy or the helpless or the depressed. Do we see Jesus in these people? Do we consider ways to help them? Sometimes the most valuable help we can offer, the most critical service we can render, is to listen to them, acknowledge them, and honor their dignity as our brothers and sisters.

PRAY THIS

Father of the helpless,
help me to help all who need whatever I can give.
Open my heart
and open my arms
to help carry the burdens of others when I can.
Give me the courage to say "yes" when I'd rather say "no."
Grant me the generosity to say "I will" when I'd rather say
"I'd rather not."
Guide me to be more like Jesus,
one who opened his arms to others
with a boundless love I can only hope to imitate.
In this way of living and loving,
may I draw closer to you by drawing closer to those you love,
expressing in my own imperfect way
your perfect love for your creation.
And may all this help me ultimately
to gain admittance to your heavenly kingdom
where I can continue to help those in need.
Amen.

CHAPTER 12

PASS THE PEACE, PLEASE

Rejoice with those who rejoice, weep with those who
weep. Have the same regard for one another;
do not be haughty but associate with the lowly;
do not be wise in your own estimation.
Do not repay anyone evil for evil;
be concerned for what is noble in the sight of all.
If possible, on your part, live at peace with all.
—Romans 12:15-18

In 2019, a young Catholic named Mike Jordan Laskey wrote about the phenomenon of social media, including the trend of Catholics who post on Twitter. He wasn't impressed. He noted, "Catholic Twitter attracts those with the sharpest opinions and loudest voices like moths to a porch light. Every conflict is heightened, every emotion intensified."

He offered some advice about dealing with the onslaught—mostly, he suggested being selective about what you read and being willing, at all times, to turn off the computer and walk away. He concluded with some wisdom from another writer, Simcha Fisher:

Everyone wants to imitate Jesus in the one time e showed some temper with the whip in the temple. Dude, you are not Jesus. It's a much safer bet to imitate him in the other 99 percent of the Gospels, like when he preached the good news, when he fed his sheep, when he gave over his body, and when he fixed his eyes firmly on the Father and then told us to do the same.[21]

Can I hear an Amen?

Now you're probably wondering: "Okay. Fine. But what does this have to do with me loving my neighbor and living that extraordinary life that I really want?"

Short answer: everything.

Longer answer: the little ecosystem that is social media, and notably Twitter, encourages us to be as uncharitable, merciless, judgmental, and brutally unkind as humanly possible just to make a point. It's symptomatic of our larger culture, I think, where the thrust and parry of public discourse is intended to draw blood. It's sport.

And it's wrong.

To put it bluntly: you don't love your neighbor by ruthlessly impaling him on your sword.

In fact, as I often tell people when I talk about the world of social media, some of the best advice to follow is found in a surprising place: the Garden of Gethsemane, when the crowd came to arrest Jesus. One of Jesus' followers came to his defense, but Jesus told him to put away his sword (see Matthew 26:52). You don't love someone with a clenched fist. And you don't win them over to the gospel with a sharp point, buried in their ribs.

You certainly don't make your life extraordinary by being a jerk. Being a jerk, after all, is easy. Try something hard.

Try forgiving. Try looking for the best in people, not the worst. Try respecting their point of view, even if you disagree, even if you hate it. Try speaking less and listening more.

Try . . . oh, I don't know . . . *peace*. Yes. Give peace a chance. It worked pretty well for Jesus.

His emphasis on peace is something that always strikes me when I read the Gospel passage about Jesus sending his followers into the world to begin their ministry. It seems like he's sending them empty-handed—the Gospel describes the things they are supposed to leave behind, including money and an extra pair of sandals (see Luke 10:4).

But no. He tells them to go bearing one simple message: "Peace." Jesus tells them. "Into whatever house you enter, first say, 'Peace to this household'" (Luke 10:5).

Peace.

It is also the first word he will say to them after the resurrection, when he appears in the upper room. And it is the great message he is asking them—and asking us—to carry into the world.

Carry no sack, no money, no sandals.

Carry, instead, peace.

Two thousand years later, I'm not sure we've done a very good job of following his command. Whatever else there may be in the world these days, there is very little peace. And I'm not speaking only of the absence of war—though God knows, we don't lack for that.

I'm thinking about the countless conflicts that erupt in our daily lives. Between husbands and wives. Between parents and children. Between neighbors. Between coworkers. Even between strangers on the street. (Honestly, I can tell you: some of the fiercest battles I've seen are waged among people driving cars on Queens Boulevard.)

But how often do we put those aside and say to people in our lives, "Peace"?

How often do we make peace our mission—and our message?

How often do we try to see Christ in the faces of those we do not understand or in those with whom we disagree?

How often do we put away the sword?

The writer Anthony de Mello tells the story of a man whose marriage was in trouble. He sought some advice from a spiritual master. The master told him, "You must learn to listen to your wife." The man took the advice to heart and returned several weeks later and said he'd learned to listen to every word his wife was saying.

The master smiled and said, "Good. Now go home and listen to every word she isn't saying."

I think if more of us did that—not just with our spouses, but with each other—it might be a beginning, a first step, toward making peace a reality. Because to listen that way means you don't have the last word. In fact, it makes Christ's first word the last word. *Peace.*

It means that he asks of us a kind of humility and attentiveness to one another.

It is a way of going into the world with nothing—except what really matters—because, in truth, the detachment that

Jesus is demanding isn't just a detachment from things (though that's a really good start). It is a detachment from ourselves. It is separating from our own pride, our own ego, our own sense of entitlement, our own feeling that we always have to be right.

It is taking with us nothing but what we are—stripped of what we pretend to be, divested of what we own and all that we use to impress people.

It is putting that aside and carrying forth just one message, in Christ's name: peace.

And in doing that, we're doing something we should be trying to do anyway.

We are loving our neighbor.

It begins with walking away from a fight—whether online or over the dinner table—and believing the best of others, not the worst. And out of that, we defuse tension and build respect.

We give peace a chance.

And we give something else a chance too: a better, fuller, gentler, extraordinary life.

CONSIDER THIS

To avoid rash judgment, everyone should be careful to interpret insofar as possible his neighbor's thoughts, words, and deeds in a favorable way:

> Every good Christian ought to be more ready to give a favorable interpretation to another's statement than to condemn it. But if he cannot do so, let him ask how the other understands it. And if the latter understands it badly, let the former correct him with love. If that does not suffice, let the Christian try all suitable ways to bring the other to a correct interpretation so that he may be saved.
>
> —*Catechism*[22]

When you are in the midst of any task, ask yourself, "Is what I am doing building up or tearing down?" In asking this question I think of St. Paul's admonition in Ephesians to "say only what will help to build others up and meet their needs" (4:29, NIrV). Now that doesn't mean that we don't speak the truth to evil or sin. Jesus himself was quite outspoken in his attacks on hypocrisy and sin. In that sense we are building up by tearing down, when we tear down evil and replace it with the good. But my admonition is more to avoid at all times the "attack ad" mentality that sadly permeates much of our public discourse today. One way in which this plays out positively is trying to communicate as much as we can what it is we are "for" rather than what we are "against."

I offer a special saint in the teachings and person of one of the great doctors of the Church, St. Therese of Lisieux and her "little way" for us communicators who serve the prophetic mission of the Church. . . In her "little way" she tells us to first live out our days with confidence in God's love and to recognize that each day is a gift in which one's life can make a difference by the way we choose to live it. Out of this comes the admonition to see every little task or moment in life as an opportunity to make concrete the love of God. Think about that in terms of what we do. Every news story, every video, every blog post, every tweet or email or response to comment boxes can become an opportunity to manifest God's love if we commit ourselves to loving.

—Bishop Christopher Coyne[23]

TRY THIS

It's only natural to want to have the last word. In any argument, everybody wants to be right. We all want to win and shut down those we think are wrong. But what if you make the choice not to? What if you choose to encourage something like peace?

The reality is that not every argument, debate, or discussion needs a winner. And if there's a winner, it doesn't necessarily have to be you. Sometimes the most important and lasting victory is made on behalf of patience. It is made for compassion. For empathy. For respect. For tolerance. Consider just making a point and walking away. Put away the sword or drop the stones in your hand. Discussions don't have to escalate into nuclear warfare (and in the dangerous world of social media, they often do!). We should avoid labeling, name-calling, and diminishing others by pasting a simplistic label on their forehead. We are all—every one of us—far more complicated and beautiful than that.

Nurture peace. Encourage respect. As Bishop Coyne put it, work on building up, not tearing down. Try that. You may be shocked at how much better it makes you feel—and how it might even stun others into trying to do the same.

PRAY THIS

Father,
your Son once called peacemakers "blessed."
How I long to be that!
Teach me to walk in the way of peace,
to be its instrument, its carrier, its messenger.
Ease my anger,
heal my frustrations,
silence my sometimes bitter tongue.
Keep me always aware of the Eden you long the world to be:
a place of tranquility and perfection and harmony.
Hear with me, to help me listen better.
Watch with me, to help me see more clearly.
Walk with me, to remind me that we need to walk with others,
no matter how hard the road.

May I always work, not to tear down, but to build up,
so that I may work joyfully to build up your kingdom on earth
and one day dwell forever in the company of the Prince of
Peace.
Amen.

CHAPTER 13

WE'RE ALL IN THIS TOGETHER

This is my commandment: love one another as I love you.
No one has greater love than this,
to lay down one's life for one's friends.
—John 15:12-13

"Love one another." It all comes back to that, doesn't it? In one way or another, the heart and soul of the Christian life—and the thread that we follow to come, at last, to an *extraordinary* life—involves being able to love. And being *willing* to love.

Part of that also involves realizing that love is more than an emotion or a feeling or a sentiment. As so many have said over the generations, love is a choice. And it is a choice with a powerful impact that can affect more than just one person.

One thing history has taught us again and again—whether it's been the struggle of a people to find their way out of Egypt or the sacrifices made to win a world war or the catchy theme song of a Disney high school musical—is that we're all in this together.

Yes. We are.

Let me tell you about a young woman named Tamara Fowler and her parents.

Tamara Fowler lived outside Atlanta and was engaged to get married. About a month before her wedding, Tamara decided to break off her engagement, and she called off the wedding. As you might imagine, this caused a few problems. Her parents, Carol and Willie Fowler, had sunk thousands of dollars into planning a dinner reception for two hundred guests at Atlanta's Villa Christina restaurant. The Fowlers were heartbroken for a lot of reasons—not the least of them being that the event was already paid for.

The father of the bride thought about the situation, talked it over with his wife, and prayed about it one night before going to bed.

The next morning, he later said, he knew what they had to do.

And what they did made news around the country.

The Fowlers decided to go on with the dinner as planned—but not with the original guest list. They invited, instead, a different group: two hundred men, women, and children who were homeless.

The Fowlers called a nonprofit organization in Atlanta called Hosea Feed the Hungry. The woman who picked up the phone later said she was so shocked, she thought it was a prank call. The Fowlers arranged a meeting and explained what they wanted to do. They told the woman at Hosea that they especially wanted to help children—at the time, according to one statistic, 70 percent of the homeless in Atlanta were kids—so they set out to make it a reality.

And so, on a September afternoon, buses brought dozens of needy people to one of the premier wedding venues in Atlanta. Children had space outside to run and play. Face painters and jugglers were hired to entertain them.

The kids, it turned out, had to be shown how to eat hors d'oeuvres and how to use the right fork. They weren't used to eating off of fine china. They had never experienced anything like it before.

And at evening's end, the caterer was amazed. For the first time, she said, at the end of a big wedding, there were no leftovers. Every plate was clean.

For a little while, people who otherwise felt overlooked, discarded, and helpless did not go hungry.

They were given an immeasurable gift: the gift of dignity.

It is a gift, the Gospels remind us, that each of us is called to share with those struggling with the hard reality of a hard life. We cannot escape the urgent commandment to love one another—particularly the poor.

More than dignity, though, the Fowlers gave those people something even more elusive. They offered them a sense of belonging. They were welcomed and included in a world they'd only imagined. The implicit message: yes, we're all in this together.

I'm reminded of the story of the rich man and Lazarus, one of the parables in Luke that Jesus tells his followers as he is making his journey to Jerusalem. Lazarus, you'll remember, had spent his days begging outside the house of the rich man, who ignored him. Lazarus, of course, got his reward in the end, enjoying life in paradise; the rich man faced a very different, and very hot, fate.

The lesson is pretty straightforward: care for the poor. Remember the helpless. Don't step over people to enjoy the life you want. Be charitable. Be generous. Give.

But the parable of the rich man and Lazarus also tells us something else: sometimes the most serious sin we can commit isn't an action. It's inaction. The rich man is damned, not for what he did, but for what he didn't do. He continually saw Lazarus suffering and did nothing. We are left to conclude that this was his great sin.

And we are left to ask ourselves: is it also ours?

Do we see a need and ignore it?

Do we see a problem and step over it?

Do we see heartbreak and desperation and then do nothing to alleviate it?

Do we fail to see in our suffering brothers and sisters the face of Christ?

Whenever we pray the *Confiteor* at Mass, the "I Confess," we ask mercy for "what I have done and what I have failed to do."

What have we failed to do?

If we were in the Fowlers' shoes, what would we do?

I think it's a great example of people who took lemons and decided to make lemonade—but then created something infinitely sweeter.

They made the world remember those who are often forgotten.

For a couple of hours, they gave a kind of home to people who had none—a place of security and plenty. They treated people who are usually overlooked and forgotten as brothers and sisters who deserve to be remembered.

They showed the world what it means to love one another. They reminded anyone who was paying attention that we are not isolated, cut off, locked away from one another. The human condition is the condition of *all* humans. We're all in this together. What can we do?

The Fowlers may have thought what they did wasn't all that exceptional. But it was. I can imagine a lot of people who would be heartbroken, angry, even bitter about spending thousands of dollars for an expensive event, only to have it upended at the last minute. But the Fowlers found a better way—a more excellent way, as St. Paul might put it: a way of love.

So it is for all of us at one time or another. The world is unjust. Hearts will break. Plans will shatter. Planned happy endings will be changed. It ain't fair. And it hurts. A lot.

How do we respond?

CONSIDER THIS

When you love people, you see all the good in them, all the Christ in them. God sees Christ, his Son, in us and loves us. And so we should see Christ in others, *and nothing else*, and love them. There can never be enough of it. There can never be enough thinking about it.

—Dorothy Day[24]

Love is an "action word." It means we have to "do" something. So our Christian love must be expressed in concrete works of service to our brothers and sisters.

Love means serving all those people who need our help. It means feeding the hungry, clothing the naked. Love heals the sick and comforts the dying.

This love is what makes our Christian participation in society different. We are not just "do-gooders" or only humanitarians.

What makes Christians different is that we know that every person is truly our brother or our sister, created in the image of God. . . .

Through our works of charity and mercy, we show the love of God to those in need. By our love, we show to our society that no one is outside the love and care of God.

We are all here to serve. We are all here to give ourselves to others. We are all here to help one another carry the burdens that we all have in this life.

—Archbishop Jose Gomez[25]

The Greek word *dikaiosune*—most commonly translated as "righteousness" or "justice"—appears pervasively throughout both the Gospels and Greek translations of the Hebrew Bible. It is the unifying ethos of the Law as given on Sinai and fulfilled by Jesus, and it is inherently relational. It is to be in right relationship with God, with self, and with neighbor.

Our salvation is not a purely individual matter. We need the Church. We need relationships that challenge our sinfulness, encourage our virtue, and advance the cause of *dikaiosune* across our many human institutions. We are necessarily a community of disciples. We need each other, focused on Christ who unifies us into a single mystical body, if we have any hope for personal redemption and societal transformation. Organized religion isn't obsolete because humans haven't stopped needing one another. I need you in the pew next to me.

—Michael Bayer, Chicago, Illinois

TRY THIS

What do we see when we look into the eyes of others? Too often we're tempted to see basic types: old, young, male, female, rich, poor, etc. Our culture encourages us to affix labels and jump to conclusions.

But what if we didn't?

A challenging exercise can be to try to see the world not with our eyes but with God's. What do we think he sees when he gazes at us? I don't think he views limitations; I like to think he sees possibilities. He doesn't see what we aren't, but what we are. And perhaps what we can be. To return to the phrase I used at the beginning, he sees all that we can be. And he sees it with a father's love and concern.

While we can't easily put ourselves into God's shoes (or, maybe, sandals), we can try to look at those around us as siblings walking the same journey. We all struggle. We stumble. We strive. We hurt.

A familiar aphorism puts it this way: "Be kind. For everyone you meet is fighting a battle you know nothing about."

Each of us can attest to that, I think, and remember all the battles we've waged—and ones that are still going on.

Battles for justice. For serenity. For hope. For a future. Try to remember: it's the same for everyone, in one way or another.

Remember this too: we're all in this together.

PRAY THIS

Dear Father of unfailing love,
help me to never fail in my love for others.
In times of mistrust or fear,
loneliness or anxiety,
open my heart to see the blessing of my brothers and sisters.
May I always remember that we are all
made in your image,
every one of us,
and that we share some spark of the divine.
Father of unity and hope,
teach me how to walk with others
in closeness, in solidarity, in faith, and in trust.
Let me see them as companions on the journey
so that we can grow closer to one another
and, with your grace, grow closer to you.
Amen.

CHAPTER 14

THE HARDEST THING TO DO

You have heard that it was said, "You shall love your
neighbor and hate your enemy." But I say to you,
love your enemies, and pray for those who persecute you,
that you may be children of your heavenly Father.
—Matthew 5:43-45

This wasn't quite the reaction I expected.

On Ash Wednesday of 2008, I climbed into the pulpit at my parish in Queens to deliver my first homily for that occasion, just nine months after my ordination. As usual for Ash Wednesday, the church was packed—standing room only, with close to a thousand people. They just wanted to get ashes. They didn't care what I was going to say.

But after the Gospel, I delivered a stem-winder about creating new ways to give up things for Lent. I thought I'd offer the people in the pews a provocative challenge, a new and audacious thing to pray during this season of prayer and sacrifice.

"Try praying for someone you don't know," I offered. "Better yet, pray for someone you don't like. Try praying for an enemy." Dramatic pause. "When was the last time anyone here prayed for Osama bin Laden?"

In unison, a thousand people gasped.

Yeah. That wasn't what I expected.

After Mass, I greeted people at the door of the church and heard some polite comments of "Nice homily, deacon" and "You gave me something to think about."

But a couple of people winced. "I don't know about that praying for bin Laden part," one woman said, squinting, pulling her hand from me as I shook it. "I'm not holy enough to do that." I smiled. "That's what Lent is all about," I reassured her. "It's trying to get that holy!"

When another parishioner expressed misgivings about the theology behind my suggestion, I offered, "Hey, it's not my idea. It's Jesus': love your enemies and pray for your persecutors. We all need to try to get there." He nodded but I could tell he didn't quite believe it.

I'm not sure how many Christians really, truly accept the notion of loving our enemies. It sounds good on paper and has a nice ring to it when it's proclaimed on Sunday morning. But it just might be one of the hardest teachings in all of Scripture.

I'll admit: I'm not that good at this myself. I have a long list of people ahead of Osama bin Laden for whom I regularly pray. I have friends who are sick with cancer and people who have asked me to pray for loved ones who are out of work or facing some sort of crisis. The enemies and persecutors are much further down my list.

Besides, how on earth can you *love* someone who hates you? And *pray* for them? Aren't there more deserving people?

Well, here's a reality check: nobody said being a Christian was easy.

But when it comes to loving our neighbor and being all we can be, we need to make the effort. We need to start walking that path—toward healing, toward wholeness, toward *holiness*. Where to start?

It begins with learning how to forgive—unbuckling the hook of hate and just walking away from it.

Several years ago, the *Columbus Dispatch* newspaper in Ohio printed a story about a First Communion—but it's one unlike any other you may have heard. It says something beautiful about the power of the Eucharist, the Bread of Life. But it is also a story of qualities in short supply in our world today: forgiveness and reconciliation.

The story began on a cold night in December of 1979. A sixteen-year-old boy named Ron McClary was at a convenience store in Columbus when police officer Tom Hayes spotted him. He realized the boy was violating a local curfew. When Hayes tried to arrest him, McClary resisted. In a split-second decision, the teenager made the biggest mistake of his young life. He pulled out a gun and shot Tom Hayes in the back.

Officer Hayes survived, but barely.

The day after the shooting, a priest friend of the officer, Fr. Kevin Lutz, visited Hayes in the hospital. Officer Hayes told the priest he was afraid of dying. Fr. Lutz asked him if he was able to forgive the boy who had shot him.

Officer Hayes told him: "I don't want to go before almighty God with hatred in my heart. I prayed I would go to heaven and that he would too."

Ron McClary was arrested and tried as an adult. He spent twenty-four years behind bars.

Tom Hayes spent the rest of his life paralyzed from the waist down. He endured bedsores, catheters, infections, and even a leg amputation. But not a day went by that he didn't pray for Ron McClary.

This went on for over three decades, until Officer Hayes died in January of 2011. Shortly afterward, his friend Fr. Lutz decided to find out what had happened to the boy who had shot him.

He found Ron McClary living in poverty in a small apartment in Columbus. The teenager had grown into a middle-aged man, crippled by multiple sclerosis. Fr. Lutz told him who he was and told him what had happened to Officer Hayes. He said that the paralyzed policeman had spent his life praying for him. He also told him he had forgiven him. McClary, deeply moved, invited him to come back and to keep talking. And Fr. Lutz did. McClary had difficulty communicating, but after many weeks he made one thing clear: he wanted to be baptized. Fr. Lutz baptized him in his home, using a simple coffee cup.

And so it happened that shortly after, Ron McClary was taken by stretcher to Holy Family Church in Columbus. Waiting for him were Fr. Lutz and Mary Hayes, Tom Hayes' widow. Fr. Lutz had called her the night before to tell her Ron's story and invite her to the Mass. She wasn't sure she could find the strength to be there. Her husband, she said, was a bigger person than she was. But she knew what he would have wanted, and she went to the church that morning. It was, she said, her greatest test as a Christian. She was there as Ron McClary received his First Communion. Then, a few moments later,

Mary Hayes bent down and whispered to McClary the words her husband never had a chance to say: "I forgive you."[26]

When I first heard that story, I was humbled and ashamed. If Tom Hayes could do that, what about me?

Throughout the Gospels, Jesus asks a lot of his followers.

Turn the other cheek. Give away your cloak. Love your enemies and pray for your persecutors.

Think about that. Run through an inventory in your mind. I'm not talking about the bin Ladens in your life; I'm thinking a little smaller.

Consider all the people who have hurt you. Those who have lied to you. Stabbed you in the back. Remember the ones who spread rumors about you that were untrue. Those who have gossiped about you or judged you or mocked you or bullied you.

Consider the friend you trusted who betrayed you. The coworker who broke a confidence. The person whose name you'd rather forget who wounded you or disrespected you or took advantage of you or even abused you. Look back on all the people in your life who have left bruises and scars with a word or a look or a touch.

Now imagine doing what Jesus commands.

Love them.

Love them and pray for them.

Pray for their good. Pray that grace will come into their lives. Pray that their eyes may be opened and their hearts may be healed. Because the chances are, if someone has hurt you or persecuted you or brought some unfathomable pain into your life, it's probably because someone once did the same to them.

It is a vicious cycle. As Shakespeare put it, "Sin will pluck on sin." Or as a former colleague of mine used to say, "Hurt people hurt people."

And that fundamental truth of our humanity—that the cycle just keeps going—may be one reason why Jesus tells his followers, in effect: "Stop. Enough. Break the cycle. Let it go."

Love your enemies and pray for your persecutors.

If anyone still has any doubts about how to do that, look no further than the cross. Jesus spent his last hours in agony but loved and forgave those who killed him and prayed on their behalf.

He showed how it is done.

Tom Hayes showed how it is done.

Our prayer needs to be that we will learn from examples like that—discovering in our own hearts how to give mercy to the merciless and forgiveness to the unforgiving, and to pray for the well-being of all who do not wish us well.

Give thanks to God for giving us this world that we share and this humanity that we share, in all our imperfections.

Give praise to him for making us beings who wonder and love and learn and create.

Never let a day go by without whispering a simple prayer of gratitude for that and for so much more.

And then let us treat those around us the way that God treats them—with respect and delight and love. We need to give thanks to God and give dignity to his children wherever we find them.

And the result? Of course: an extraordinary life.

CONSIDER THIS

When the opportunity presents itself for you to defeat your enemy, that is the time which you must not do it. There will come a time, in many instances, when the person who hates you most, the person who has misused you most, the person who has gossiped about you most, the person who has spread false rumors about you most, there will come a time when you will have an opportunity to defeat that person. It might be in terms of a recommendation for a job; it might be in terms of helping that person to make some move in life. That's the time you must not do it. That is the meaning of love.

In the final analysis, love is not this sentimental something that we talk about. It's not merely an emotional something. Love is creative, understanding goodwill for all men. It is the refusal to defeat any individual. When you rise to the level of love, of its great beauty and power, you seek only to defeat evil systems. Individuals who happen to be caught up in that system, you love, but you seek to defeat the system.

—Dr. Martin Luther King, Jr.[27]

Jesus' biggest challenge to us is to love our enemies. On death row, I encountered the enemy—those considered so irredeemable by our society that even our Supreme Court has made it legal to kill them. For twenty years now, I've been visiting people on death row, and I have accompanied six human beings to their deaths. As each has been killed, I have told them to look at me. I want them to see a loving face when they die. I want my face to carry the love that tells them that they and every one of us are worth more than our most terrible acts.

—Sr. Helen Prejean[28]

TRY THIS

The surest way to conquer an enemy, at least in your own heart, is also the simplest: pray.

Pray that those who lack empathy will learn compassion. Pray that those who cause pain will learn gentleness. Pray that God will move hearts to live differently, believe differently, and behave differently.

And pray too for the strength to withstand everything the enemy throws at you.

The 12-step recovery group Al-Anon, created to support and help families and friends of alcoholics, teaches detachment. "We are not responsible for another person's disease or recovery from it," one brochure puts it. "Detachment allows us to let go of our obsession with another's behavior and begin to lead happier and more manageable lives, lives with dignity and rights, lives guided by a Power greater than ourselves. We can still love the person without liking the behavior."[29]

I think this gets to the root of what it means to love our enemies and pray for our persecutors.

If you ask God for nothing else, pray for a spirit of detachment from those who wound you—and pray, above all, for peace.

PRAY THIS

Dear God,
in times of confusion or doubt,
of suffering and despair,
I turn to you for solace and hope.
Teach me how to love the ones I find unlovable—
(even if the one I find unlovable at times is myself).
Help me see the dignity of every life,
the possibility of every soul,
the dreams of every mind,
that I may forgive, honor, detach,
and—ultimately—love.
Bring me the gift of peace.
I offer this prayer knowing that I am seeking to do
the impossible
or what seems, at least, impossible to me.
But I know that you make all things possible,
and I honor and love all that you are
and all that you have made possible for me.
Help me always to stay close to you,
to your Son, Jesus Christ,
to our mother, Mary,
and to your comforting Holy Spirit.
Now and always,
Amen.

THE WORLD TURNED UPSIDE DOWN

I started this book at a challenging moment, as the coronavirus pandemic was just beginning in the spring of 2020.

A couple of times a day, I have had to get up from my desk, go to the window, and check.

Yes. New York City is still there.

But it feels like it isn't. Life in lockdown is like that. The world seems to have stopped, and nothing is quite what it was.

I've been working from home. The office building in Manhattan where I work as a writer and editor for Catholic Near East Welfare Association (CNEWA) has closed for the foreseeable future, so I'm doing what I can from my laptop here in Queens.

It's a strange time to be a New Yorker. The streets are deserted. The sidewalks are empty. The store shelves are barren. The local bagel shop is struggling to stay open. The Italian restaurant just across the street from our church—the place where families have gathered for decades after baptisms and First Communions and funerals—is shuttered (though it is still offering takeout and delivery, so we're not being deprived of Carmine's pasta).

And then there is the church itself, a stone landmark on Queens Boulevard, standing there now, strangely unused. Yet the bells still toll for the Angelus. They remind us of a time before—before the lights were dimmed and the doors were locked. They remind us of a time when voices filled the air, incense wreathed the altar, that vast space inside teemed with life as light streamed through the stained glass windows, and elderly women with rosaries made their way around the church, whispering prayers at the Stations of the Cross or slipping a folded piece of paper under the foot of St. Jude, with a prayer intention scrawled on the back of a grocery list.

Now that's gone.

So much has changed.

My wife and I are self-quarantined in our apartment several blocks away. Now and then I venture out to buy some milk or mail a bill. Early on, I bravely visited my barber for a haircut. "How's business?" I asked as he draped a cloth around my shoulders. He shrugged. He explained, in his thick Russian accent, "Yesterday, two people. Day before, one. Today, you. What you gonna do?" I asked him if he was going to close. "Nah. Forty years, 365 days open, never close. Never."

"Never" soon became history. Not long after, the governor ordered beauty salons and barbershops closed.

The day I had my haircut, I walked past people wearing masks and rubber gloves. People don't talk if they don't have to. They scurry, wanting to get back home as quickly as possible.

So much has changed.

That extends to my ministry too. With a lot of things canceled—Masses, sacraments, parish meetings—familiar patterns are broken. It's easy to feel disconnected from the life of the parish.

But in the midst of all that, we are reminded that being church is larger than being *in* church. Faith endures.

It is there every morning when I click on my computer and behold an astonishing world of prayer, resilience, and hope. I scroll through social media and am amazed. There is a priest offering Confession in a parking lot in Maryland; another priest is offering Eucharistic Adoration from the window of his church in Massachusetts; there are people creating prayer groups, Rosary societies, online perpetual Adoration. Parents are sharing ideas for homeschooling, catechesis, ways of watching Mass together through Face-Time or Skype.

So much has changed.

But I'm realizing too that much has not.

We are still the body of Christ. We are doing our level best to support one another, pray with one another, encourage one another, and worship the God we love.

In my life as a deacon—a deacon who is, not insignificantly, engaged in a ministry of communications—that means sharing as many of these stories as possible on my blog, connecting readers to the larger Church, and helping all of us realize we are not alone.

We aren't. Really. Grace is everywhere—streaming to us across Twitter and Facebook and YouTube if only we take the time to look for it.

We need to look. This pandemic is forcing most of us to watch the world through a screen and over a keyboard.

What do we see?

Mr. Rogers used to tell people during times of turmoil, "Look for the helpers." We need to look for them, even more, these days; they can be harder to spot because so many are at home, hidden. But in quiet but resolute ways, they can remind us that the world isn't entirely composed of hoarders who have to grab that last roll of Charmin.

There's the professional concert pianist who was unable to attend a conference out of town, so he set up a portable piano outside to play for his neighbors.

There's the group of high school students who found their spring concert canceled, so they recorded a rendition of "Over the Rainbow" via Skype, and the whole thing went—really—viral, uplifting and charming thousands around the world.

Thoughtful, prayerful, enterprising people connected through wires and antennae—these are people to give us hope. And we need that.

And out of this too we can find a way of life that is, truly, extraordinary.

I've told people often during these weeks: this is a great time to turn more to prayer.

Seek out sacred readings, and study the lives of the saints—they have much to teach us right now about persistence, resilience, and faith.

And, significantly, focus on the domestic church of the family. You want to love your neighbor? Start with the one who sits across from you at the kitchen table.

In his beautiful exhortation The Joy of the Gospel, Pope Francis wrote, "Each of us should find ways to communicate Jesus wherever we are. All of us are called to offer others an explicit witness to the saving love of the Lord, who despite our imperfections offers us his closeness, his word and his strength, and gives meaning to our lives" (121).

We do it here and now. With patience. With prayer. With attention.

We do it with generosity.

We do it with love.

So often, we take those around us for granted. Well, I think these days are a time to see them anew. At this moment, they are more than siblings or spouses or kids doing classes on Zoom.

They are our church—our domestic church.

We need to cherish that. And find ways in that church "to communicate Jesus." Give generously. Forgive tenderly. Share selflessly. Pray together in solidarity and hope.

We all need that.

Not long after this crisis began, I texted a friend, "Maybe we are being given this time to realize that being Catholic Christian isn't just about what we receive; it's also about what we give."

Maybe, I explained, this is a moment for us to pause and consider other ways of being Catholic.

Even in times of quarantine and solitude, we have much to give the world. I think of our cloistered brothers and sisters around the world who unite their prayers with ours, and wonder if this is a moment for us to be more intimately connected with them—and, by extension, with others who are isolated or imprisoned, held captive by weakness, illness, or persecution.

The world outside my apartment window is still there. (I just checked.)

We need to appreciate that wonder for the miracle that it is—and give thanks to the One who has made it possible.

It is an invitation and a promise. Something awaits us. We shouldn't waste a moment we are given.

Take up the challenge. Accept the invitation. Love God. Love neighbor.

Dare to do that, and we can dare to be all that we can be.

NOTES

1. Pope Benedict, Address to the German Pilgrims Who Had Come to Rome for the Inauguration Ceremony of the Pontificate, April 25, 2005, http://www.vatican.va/content/benedict-xvi/en/speeches/2005/april/documents/hf_ben-xvi_spe_20050425_german-pilgrims.html.
2. Hendry Chadwick, trans., *Saint Augustine's Confessions* (New York: Oxford University Press, 1991), 50.
3. Clare Carlisle, *Philosopher of the Heart: The Restless Life of Søren Kierkegaard* (New York: Farrar, Straus and Giroux, 2020), 15.
4. J. R. R. Tolkien, *The Letters of J. R. R. Tolkien,* ed. Humphrey Carpenter (Boston: Mariner Books, 2000), 53.
5. Mother Teresa, *In the Heart of the World: Thoughts, Stories, and Prayers* (Novato, CA: New World Library, 1997), 20.
6. Pope Francis, *Gaudete et Exsultate* [Rejoice and Be Glad], March 19, 2018, 1, 9, http://www.vatican.va/content/francesco/en/apost_exhortations/documents/papa-francesco_esortazione-ap_20180319_gaudete-et-exsultate.html.
7. Pope John Paul II, Letter to Artists, April 4, 1999, 2, http://www.vatican.va/content/john-paul-ii/en/letters/1999/documents/hf_jp-ii_let_23041999_artists.html.

8. Letter to Artists, 1.

9. St. Maria Faustina Kowalska, *Diary of Saint Maria Kowalska: Divine Mercy in My Soul* (Stockbridge, MA: Marian Press, 2005), no. 148.

10. Dorothy Day, *The Long Loneliness: The Autobiography of the Legendary Social Activist* (New York, NY: Harper and Row Publishers, 1952), 10.

11. Pope Francis, General Audience, November 13, 2013, 1, http://www.vatican.va/content/francesco/en/audiences/2013/documents/papa-francesco_20131113_udienza-generale.html.

12. St. Benedict, *The Rule of St. Benedict* (Mineola, NY: Dover Publications, 2007), 42.

13. Jim Graves, "My Uncle, Fulton Sheen," *Catholic World Report*, September 25, 2012, https://www.catholicworldreport.com/2012/09/25/my-uncle-fulton-sheen/.

14. Thomas Merton, ed. Naomi Burton, Brother Patrick Hart, and James Laughlin, *The Asian Journal of Thomas Merton* (New York: New Directions Publishing, 1975), 308.

15. Simon Porter, *Heaven on Earth* (Trowbridge, United Kingdom: Paragon Publishing, 2017), 17.

16. Chris Tiegreen, *The One Year Walk with God Devotional: Wisdom from the Bible to Renew Your Mind* (Carol Stream, IL: Tyndale House, 2004).

17. Pope Francis, *Evangelii Gaudium* [The Joy of the Gospel], November 24, 2013, 10, http://www.vatican .va/content/francesco/en/apost_exhortations/ documents/papa-francesco _esortazione-ap_20131124_evangelii-gaudium.html.

18. Charles C. Camosy, "Gaffigan: If Tumor Was a Test of Faith, I Passed ... But Not with Flying Colors," *Crux*, August 26, 2019, https://cruxnow.com/ interviews/2019/08/comedy-writer-if-tumor-was-a-test-of-faith-i-passed-but-not-with-flying-colors/.

19. Pope Francis, Homily, September 25, 2015, http:// www.vatican.va/content/francesco/en/homilies/2015/ documents/papa-francesco_20150925_usa-ome-lia-nyc.html.

20. Pope Francis, Homily.

21. Mike Jordan Laskey, "Hateful Things Flood Catholic Twitter Every Day. It's Still Worth Saving," *National Catholic Reporter*, October 24, 2019, https://www .ncronline.org/news/opinion/young-voices/hateful-things-flood-catholic-twitter-every-day-its-still-worth-saving.

22. *Catechism*, 2478 (St. Ignatius of Loyola, *Spiritual Exercises*, 22).

23. Bishop Christopher Coyne, , Homily from the Opening Mass of the Catholic Media Conference June 21, 2012, https://saltandlighttv.org/blogfeed/getpost .php?id=37668.

24. Dorothy Day, "On Pilgrimage," *The Catholic Worker*, April 1948, https://www.catholicworker.org/dorothy day/articles/467.html.

25. Archbishop Jose Gomez, "The Church Is a People of Charity," *Angelus News*, October 29, 2014, https://angelusnews.com/local/la-catholics/the-church-is-a-people-of-charity/.

26. JoAnne Viviano, "33 Years Later, Man Receives Forgiveness in Officer's Shooting," *Columbus Dispatch*, July 21, 2012, https://www.dispatch.com/article/20120721/NEWS/307219871.

27. Dr. Martin Luther King, Jr, "Loving Your Enemies," sermon , November 17, 1957, https://kinginstitute.stanford.edu/king-papers/documents/loving-your-enemies-sermon-delivered-dexter-avenue-baptist-church.

28. Sr. Helen Prejean, "Living My Prayer," *National Public Radio*, January 6, 2008, https://www.npr.org/templates/story/story.php?storyId=17845521.

29. Al-Anon, "Detachment," https://al-anon.org/pdf/S19.pdf.